THE
ONE-BOTTLE
COCKTAIL

THE
ONE-BOTTLE
COCKTAIL

More than 80 Recipes
with Fresh Ingredients
and a Single Spirit

MAGGIE HOFFMAN

Photographs by Kelly Puleio

TEN SPEED PRESS
California | New York

FOR MATT
AND MINNA
WITH LOVE

CONTENTS

Bourbon in Black,
page 166

INTRODUCTION

This happens often: You order a cocktail at a charming new restaurant or bar, and fall in love at first sip. The drink is silky and spiritous, not too sweet, and just a little bitter—the kind of cocktail that portends an excellent evening. You take another sip and ask your waiter or bartender for details. *What's in this, again? It's fantastic.*

There's bourbon, so that's a good start. You have a bottle of Maker's in your liquor cabinet. And then the bad news comes. There's also Cappelletti Amaro Sfumato Rabarbaro, and amontillado sherry, mole bitters, plus a cardamom tincture. Or maybe it's tequila and grapefruit liqueur, housemade orgeat, Cocchi Vermouth di Torino, and aquavit.

You'd better order another round, my friend, because you're never going to make that drink at home.

This happens often too: You receive a new cocktail book as a birthday or holiday gift, and every photo gets your mouth watering. You want to make a special drink for an upcoming dinner party, but as you turn page after page, you realize that would be a pricey proposition indeed. You have tequila, but not Cynar or Lillet or celery bitters. You have a bottle of gin, but a half bottle of Chartreuse is going to set you back thirty-five bucks and maraschino liqueur will run you the same. It feels insane to shell out for Bonal Gentiane-Quina and Cherry Heering when you only need a few half-ounces, and you don't even know if you'll like the drink or not.

If you've been there, this book is for you.

If you love the cocktails you've had at bars and restaurants, but don't have an extra room in your apartment for a ton of esoteric bottles, this book is for you.

If you're bored with gin and tonics or you can't really find a classic cocktail that's to your taste; if you're looking for something fresh to serve at a barbecue, birthday party, office happy hour, or bridal shower, this book is for you.

If you're going on vacation and want to drink well but pack light, this book is for you. Bon voyage!

THE RULES

Every one of the eighty-three drinks in this book calls for just one bottle. That means the vodka in your freezer, or gin, agave spirits like tequila and mezcal, rum, pisco, Cognac, bourbon, rye, or Scotch.

None of these drinks require bitters, vermouth, or liqueurs.

There's no amaro, no aperitif wine, no absinthe. Just one bottle of booze—which you might already have in your liquor cabinet or on your mantel—and ingredients you can find at your favorite grocery store. These drinks call on herbs and fruit, vegetables, spices, vinegars, honey, maple syrup, soda, and other common ingredients to build complex, unusual flavor profiles.

Cocktail historians might point out that the technical, "official" definition of a cocktail includes a base spirit, a sweetener, bitters, and water (usually of the chilly sort). So, I suppose, if we're being very literal, these are *drinks* (or sometimes highballs or sours, fizzes or smashes) and not cocktails. But there are all sorts of things that can add a bitters-like experience (and depth of flavor) to a beverage: citrus pith, say, or tea, spicy cinnamon or ginger or black pepper, or the quinine that's in your tonic water. I'm fine with calling these drinks by whatever name you want, as long as we both have something cool to sip while we argue about it.

To build this book, I reached out to some of the most creative bartenders in the Bay Area, where I live; in New York, where I started my drinks-writing career; and in Portland, where I was raised. I gathered and tested recipes from fantastic bar directors and drinks creators based in Chicago, Seattle, London, Boston, Los Angeles, Miami, and Minneapolis, among other cities. These industry stars are pros at balancing flavors and giving each drink that essential element of surprise.

BONUS DRINKS

Each chapter of *The One-Bottle Cocktail* offers recipes designed around the spirit in question: vodka, gin, tequila, bourbon, and so on. Go ahead and drink your way through each collection, but you won't be quite done by the end. There's a "Bonus Drinks" page at the end of each chapter calling out even more drinks: that is, recipes elsewhere in the book that work well with an alternate spirit and can help you make your way to the bottom of any bottle.

This base-swapping move is a common way that bartenders riff on classic cocktails: For example, a standard Negroni is made with gin (plus Campari and sweet vermouth), but some people prefer the Boulevardier, which keeps the Campari and vermouth but calls for whiskey instead of gin. The drinks are cousins, not twins; different, but both delicious.

In the "Bonus Drinks" section, you'll find my favorite swaps. For example, I love making a pitcher of the Cranberry in a Can (page 153) with rye whiskey, but it also works wonderfully with Cognac. If you're looking for more rum drinks after you've arrived at the end of the rum chapter, you'll find that the Silken Sour (page 33), which first appears with the vodka drinks, will happily adapt. Try the recipes both ways and see which you prefer.

I hope you're thirsty.

TOOLS, TRICKS, AND WHAT YOU NEED TO GET STARTED

I believe you can shake up polished, fancy bar–worthy drinks at home without emptying your wallet, so I'm not going to recommend that you do a ton of stocking up in advance. You do, though, need a handful of standard tools and ingredients. Here's how to choose them wisely.

JIGGERS AND MEASURERS

Accurate measurement can make or break your cocktails: sloppy over- or underpouring can result in a drink that's too sweet or too strong. Tall Japanese-style jiggers encourage much more accuracy than their squat American-style cousins, and often have the added bonus of markings at the ¼- and ¾-ounce line. You should *not* be eyeballing those quantities.

Those starting out might find they can avoid messy counters by using a mini angled measuring cup, such as the metal ones from OXO, instead of a jigger. You have to be vigilant about filling each measurement exactly to the line, but it'll spare you the common jigger-spillage problem.

COCKTAIL SHAKER

If you already have a cocktail shaker that you're comfortable using, congrats! If you've always struggled to unseal a mixing glass from a shaking tin, or you've battled with a vacuumed-shut three-piece cobbler shaker, I have a recommendation: go the two-part all-metal route. A Boston shaker made up of two metal tins—one large (28 ounce) and one small (18 ounce)—is easier to unseal after you've shaken your drink.

Need a quick refresher on how to do it? After you've added your measured ingredients to the smaller tin and then plopped in your ice, place the larger tin on top at a jaunty angle, then smack it to seal. Hold tight and shake, angling the tins parallel to the

floor rather than up and down. When you've thoroughly chilled the cocktail—count and make sure you're really shaking it for the recommended time!—wipe your brow and take a look at where the two tins meet. If you were looking at a compass, let's call that meeting point due south. Give the tins a smack with the heel of your hand at the point of the compass that would be marked directly east or west. Your smack will break the seal and allow the tins to separate.

Why bother to shake drinks at all—besides that you look like a badass doing it? Couldn't we just stir them with ice until cool and save ourselves some trouble? Sorry, bud, it really does make a difference. In addition to chilling a drink to its ideal temperature and adding proper dilution, shaking helps bring out the flavors and aromatic oils in herbs, fruits, or vegetables that bang around in the shaker. Plus, the process also introduces tiny bubbles that completely alter the texture of the drink in your mouth.

HAWTHORNE STRAINER

Once the drink is chilled, you've got to get it out of the shaker. Make sure your cocktail strainer fits your shaker well; there are plenty of pretty ones that are quite small, and if the strainer doesn't cover the sides of the tin you're pouring from, the unstrained drink (and maybe even some ice cubes) will tumble out.

Often, a Hawthorne strainer is enough, but when you're working with raspberry seeds, thyme leaves, pineapple threads, or other little bits, you're also going to need a . . .

FINE-MESH STRAINER

I like the conically shaped fine-mesh strainers that are just slightly bigger than a glass. A round-bottomed strainer is much more likely to drip your carefully prepared cocktail everywhere. There's no need to get too fancy here; a ten-buck set from Culina works fine. To use a fine-mesh strainer for cocktails, you'll be double-straining—just hold the ice back with your Hawthorne strainer using your dominant hand, then pour the drink through the fine-mesh strainer into the serving glass.

MUDDLER

Making drinks without liqueurs, vermouth, and bitters means you often need to extract flavor from herbs, fruits, vegetables, and spices. You're gonna get friendly with your muddler (though yes, in a pinch, you can also use a tapered French-style rolling pin or the end of a wooden spoon). Unvarnished wood or metal-and-rubber styles work fine.

Fruits and veggies can usually take a little punishment, but you need to be careful when muddling fresh herbs, especially if your muddler has teeth on the bottom. Too much mashing and you'll end up with oxidized, swampy-tasting herb paste. Just press the leaves lightly, folding them over and pressing again until they smell good. Then stop while you're ahead.

CITRUS SQUEEZER

A lever-style handheld citrus squeezer uses the magic of physics to help you squeeze juices from lemons and limes. Make sure the cut side of your citrus is facing down into the holes; you don't want the round side of the citrus to be cupped in the juicer, because then the juice will squirt up toward you. I learned from Michael Dietsch, author of *Shrubs* and *Whiskey*, to cut off the little nub on the pointy end of the lemon before squeezing to help the fruit stay in place.

ELECTRIC JUICER (AND OTHER OPTIONS)

We live in a miraculous time when you can acquire fresh carrot juice and even beet juice at many grocery stores, but some of the most vibrant flavors you can put in a drink require juices you don't often find in a bottle.

Some fruits and vegetables take kindly to citrus squeezers— you can make bright, poppingly sweet-tart pomegranate juice

by wedging a pomegranate quarter into the squeezer. (Consider changing out of your new white shirt first.)

You can add many other types of produce—like peeled fresh pears or even celery—to your food processor or blender, then strain the puree to get fresh juice that's far better than anything you can find premade.

When you need spicy-hot fresh ginger juice, the easiest move is to visit your local juice shop and ask them to sell you just a couple of ounces. If they look at you funny, just tell them I sent you. The second-easiest move is to use a masticating or centrifugal electric juicer if you have one loitering in a closet somewhere. These are really excellent effort-savers. If you don't have access to a juicer, you can thinly slice the item (or even shave it using a vegetable peeler), and either whiz it in a food processor or blender or pound the slices in a mortar and pestle before pushing against a fine-mesh strainer to extract the juice. This takes a little muscle and time, but the alternative is a disaster: shelf-stable bottled ginger juice has an acrid, sour flavor that will ruin your drinks, and commercially available ginger syrup is significantly less potent and much more sweet.

SIMPLE SYRUP: IT'S SIMPLE

Many folks are intimidated by the idea of simple syrup. It's time to get over our fears: no one wants a grainy mouthful of sugar in their drink. Plus, making simple syrup is actually crazy easy, especially if you happen to have a resealable jar (such as a mason jar) around. For 1:1 simple syrup, add equal parts sugar and hot water, seal, and shake until dissolved. Let cool before using and store for up to several weeks in the fridge. For 2:1 simple syrup, mix two parts sugar to one part hot water and proceed as above. Easy-peasy.

Your simple syrup needn't be so basic, though; many grocery stores offer entire shelves of different types of sugar. Less-processed cane, turbinado, and demerara are a few great ways to add a touch more complexity to your drinks.

HONEY AND HONEY SYRUP

Most bartenders prefer the robust flavor of raw honey over the mellow predictability of pasteurized types. Dark-colored honeys, like buckwheat, are especially fun, adding an earthy, almost smoky flavor to drinks. This profile generally fits best with barrel-aged spirits, though you can feel free to play around.

It's easier to move honey from measurer to shaker if you dilute it. Be sure to read each recipe carefully: this dilution level (and the quantity called for) makes a big difference in how sweet each drink is. If I'm only making one or two drinks, I like to mix individual portions of honey syrup right in my mini measuring cup, but if you'd like to stash a batch for multiple cocktails, be sure to store your syrup in a clean container in your fridge (and label it!).

Want to make a big, big batch? Just change the word *ounces* below to *cups*.

1:1 HONEY SYRUP Mix one part (say, 1 ounce) honey with one part (again, 1 ounce) hot water and stir until dissolved.

2:1 HONEY SYRUP Mix two parts (say, 1 ounce) honey with one part (so, ½ ounce) hot water and stir until dissolved.

3:1 HONEY SYRUP Mix three parts (say, 1½ ounces) honey with one part (you've got it, ½ ounce) hot water and stir until dissolved.

MAKING AGAVE SYRUP? Just substitute agave nectar in the proportions noted above. Same goes for maple.

EGG WHITES AND ALTERNATIVES

Many cocktails, especially sours, are traditionally crowned with fluffy, silky foam. Usually, that foam is made by shaking raw egg white into the drink (sometimes first without ice to emulsify, then with ice to chill). You'll want to use fresh eggs from a source you trust.

If you're skeeved out by raw eggs, though, or you're serving drinks to vegans, you can always substitute ¾ ounce of aquafaba for every egg white. Aquafaba is just a fancy name for the liquid in a can of chickpeas (or the cooking liquid from cooked chickpeas). Be sure to buy a low-sodium version or cook the dried chickpeas without salt to avoid throwing off the balance of your drink. Since getting aquafaba to foam up requires some really hard shaking, some people prefer to buzz it with an immersion blender instead before adding ice to the shaker.

CHILL, PLEASE

You'll serve most of the drinks in this book in tall collins glasses, squat rocks glasses, cocktail coupes, or wine glasses. (I also love Nick and Nora glasses, which look a bit like delicate, diminutive wine glasses.) You'll generally want to chill any glass that isn't going be filled with ice so that it'll help keep your drink colder longer.

Here's a clever trick I learned from Kevin Liu of the Tin Pan in Richmond, Virginia: Wet a paper towel and squeeze out any excess liquid. Wrap it around your cocktail glass and stash the wrapped glass in the freezer. It'll be properly cold in about three minutes. (You can also just fill the glass with ice water and leave it on your counter for about six minutes, if you don't have the freezer space.)

NERDS, RIGHT THIS WAY

If you really want to study and master all the moves, I recommend seeking out a general primer like Jeffrey Morgenthaler's *The Bar Book*. If you want a deeper scientific understanding about why cocktail technique matters, dive into Dave Arnold's *Liquid Intelligence*.

BEES
IN THE TRAP

MAKES 1 DRINK

I find that floral liqueurs always sit gathering dust in my liquor cabinet, and I usually prefer the flavors of fresh herbs and floral teas, anyway. There's no need to shell out for another expensive bottle when you have access to aromatic jasmine green tea and citrusy lemongrass. This smooth sour from Kaitlyn Stewart of Royal Dinette in Vancouver, British Columbia, brings them together with vodka to let the delicate flavors shine; salt and honey give the drink a round, full texture. For a strong brew, let the tea steep for about four minutes. Its robust flavor and touch of bitterness help to balance the drink.

2-inch piece fresh lemongrass

Pinch kosher salt

1½ ounces vodka

1 ounce strong-brewed jasmine green tea, cooled

½ ounce 2:1 honey syrup (page 14)

½ ounce fresh lime juice

GARNISH: 2 (4-inch) lemongrass pieces

Remove tough outer layer from lemongrass and slice into slim rings. Muddle lemongrass with salt in a cocktail shaker to break down the lemongrass's fibers and release the oils. Add vodka, cooled tea, honey syrup, and lime juice and fill the shaker with ice. Shake vigorously until well chilled, about 12 seconds. Double-strain into a chilled coupe glass. Garnish with 2 pieces of lemongrass laid on top of the glass.

WALKABOUT

MAKES 1 DRINK

Sarah Rosner of Radiator in Washington, D.C., shared this drink, which encapsulates everything there is to love about citrus season. Made with sweet, ripe tangerines, mandarins, or clementines, it pops with enough juicy orange flavor to bring you out of any cold-weather doldrums. A pinch of ground turmeric gives the cocktail a delicate savory character.

1½ ounces vodka

½ ounce 1:1 honey syrup (page 14)

1 ounce fresh tangerine or mandarin orange juice

½ ounce fresh lemon juice

Pinch ground turmeric

1½ ounces chilled club soda

GARNISH: pinch ground turmeric

Combine vodka, honey syrup, tangerine juice, lemon juice, and turmeric in a cocktail shaker and fill with ice. Shake until well chilled, about 12 seconds. Double-strain into an ice-filled collins glass, pour the soda down the side of the glass, and give it a brief, gentle stir. Sprinkle a little more turmeric on top and serve with a straw.

PURPLE FOG

MAKES 1 DRINK

This easy sour is worth making for its color alone: you've never seen a more gorgeous hue of purply magenta. Wait until the jammy Concord grapes come into season: you'll know them by their jelly-like, crazy sweet interiors, which taste just like grape jam, even when raw. Tommy Quimby of Rich Table in San Francisco keeps it simple and clean in this drink, cutting the grapes' juicy flavor with lime and vodka.

4 Concord grapes

2 ounces vodka

¾ ounce 1:1 simple syrup (page 13)

½ ounce fresh lime juice

GARNISH:
bay leaf (optional)

Muddle grapes in a cocktail shaker until well broken up. Add vodka, simple syrup, and lime juice and fill with ice. Shake until well chilled, about 12 seconds. Double-strain into a chilled coupe glass, garnishing with a bay leaf if desired.

GARDEN GNOME

MAKES 1 DRINK

Before I tasted this basil-scented concoction from Bethany Kocak of Animal in Los Angeles, I worried that a drink made with unripe tomato would be harsh, like a sour Bloody Mary. But man, was I wrong, and now I'm not sure I'll ever use green tomatoes for frying again. This cocktail is tart, delicately fruity, and softly herbal. It's perfect for a backyard brunch or pairing with a predinner snack plate.

⅓ cup chopped green (unripe) beefsteak tomato

Pinch Maldon salt

6 fresh basil leaves, torn

1½ ounces vodka

¾ ounce fresh lime juice

½ ounce 1:1 simple syrup (page 13)

Muddle tomato with salt in a cocktail shaker until liquefied. Add basil and muddle gently 5 more times. Add vodka, lime juice, and simple syrup and fill cocktail shaker with ice. Shake until well chilled, about 12 seconds. Double-strain into a chilled coupe glass.

PHUKET

MAKES 2 DRINKS

Bright, sweet mint and savory cilantro make a winning combination in refreshing Thai and Vietnamese salads, and these tender green herbs are wonderful paired in a cocktail too. For this drink, you'll whiz ripe honeydew in the blender to get it juicy with zero effort, then shake the strained melon juice with ice and all the herbs to gently bring out their vibrant flavors.

2 cups cubed honeydew

3 ounces vodka

1 ounce 1:1 simple syrup (page 13)

1 ounce fresh lime juice

16 fresh mint leaves

6 fresh cilantro sprigs

Pinch salt

GARNISH: 2 cilantro sprigs and 2 mint sprigs (optional)

Prepare 2 collins glasses by arranging a cilantro sprig vertically inside each. Combine cubed honeydew, vodka, simple syrup, and lime juice in a blender and blend until uniform. Strain through a chinois or fine-mesh strainer into a cocktail shaker. Add mint leaves, 6 cilantro sprigs, and salt and fill shaker with ice. Shake until well chilled, about 12 seconds. Add ice to prepared glasses and strain cocktail into them, garnishing with mint sprigs if desired.

EL GALLITO

MAKES ABOUT 12 DRINKS

Have you ever met a drink that also provides its own perfect snack accompaniment? This rare treasure, an umami-rich sweet-salty-smoky chipotle number from Matthew McKinley Campbell of Comal in Berkeley and A Mano in San Francisco, balances juicy pineapple with grassy green cilantro. It straddles the line between sweet and savory: a handful of cherry tomatoes tamps down the fruity flavor without pushing the drink into full-on Bloody Mary territory. The mixer is easy to prep in advance for a group, and the solids that you strain off the blended mixture become a fresh, spicy salsa that's excellent with chips. Vodka lets the drink's vivid flavors shine, but the mix is also good with reposado tequila.

25 fresh cilantro stems with leaves

2 green onions, top third of greens removed

8 cherry tomatoes

1 cup diced fresh pineapple

8 ounces lime juice

5 ounces water

4 ounces undiluted agave nectar

1 ounce adobo sauce from canned chipotles

Pinch salt

About 24 ounces vodka

GARNISH:
12 cocktail picks, each with 1 cherry tomato half

Slice cilantro and green onions into 3-inch segments, then add to a blender along with tomatoes, pineapple, lime juice, water, agave nectar, adobo sauce, and salt. Process until smooth. Strain through a chinois or fine-mesh strainer into a large measuring cup. Set aside solids to serve as a salsa, refrigerating if not serving immediately.

Measure the liquid mix (it should yield about 24 ounces) and pour into a 2-quart pitcher or resealable container along with an equal amount of vodka. If not serving right away, refrigerate for up to 3 hours.

When ready to serve, stir mixture well, then add 1½ cups ice to pitcher and give it another gentle stir. Pour into ice-filled rocks glasses and garnish each one with a speared cherry tomato half.

BEHIND THE FIELD

MAKES 1 DRINK

Arnaud Dissais of Mace in New York City muses here on the French Pearl, a gin, lime, absinthe, and mint cocktail once served at New York's Pegu Club. He riffs on the spice profile of that drink, bringing in warm star anise and swapping the mint for fresh parsley, which offers an herbal backbone and a balancing cut of bitterness. Martini lovers will like this one: together, the citrus, herbs, and spices almost taste like a good vermouth. And yes, that means you should also try this recipe with gin.

2 flat-leaf Italian parsley sprigs

2 ounces vodka

¾ ounce star anise syrup (see recipe)

½ ounce fresh lime juice

½ ounce fresh lemon juice

GARNISH: 2 fresh parsley leaves

Gently muddle parsley sprigs (just tapping and folding them a few times) in a cocktail shaker until lightly bruised. Add vodka, star anise syrup, lime juice, and lemon juice and fill with ice. Shake until well chilled, about 12 seconds. Double-strain into a chilled coupe glass. Rub the rim with a parsley leaf, then float another parsley leaf on top.

STAR ANISE SYRUP

MAKES ABOUT 6 OUNCES, ENOUGH FOR 8 DRINKS

½ cup sugar

½ cup very hot water

8 star anise pods

Combine sugar, water, and star anise in a reseal-able glass jar with a tight-fitting lid and shake until sugar dissolves. Let sit for 30 minutes. Strain through a fine-mesh strainer into a resealable container and discard star anise. Refrigerate for up to 2 weeks.

SILKEN SOUR

MAKES 1 DRINK

This subtly creamy concoction from Chicago bartender Julia Momose gets its milky-white color and luscious texture from a scoop of silken tofu. Don't expect the flavor to be savory, though. This drink is like a perfectly sour lime candy that melts in your mouth, sip after sip. Shaking the drink with ice chills it, while a second shake without ice helps every bit of the tofu blend into the cocktail. Don't skimp on the timing; give yourself a little workout and shake the drink until it's really emulsified. You can also make a delicious version with light rum.

1 ¾ ounces vodka

1 ounce 1:1 simple syrup (page 13)

¾ ounce fresh lime juice

1 tablespoon silken tofu

GARNISH: lime twist and freshly grated nutmeg

Combine vodka, simple syrup, lime juice, and tofu in a cocktail shaker and fill with ice. Shake vigorously until well chilled, about 20 seconds. Strain into one half of the shaker and discard ice and solids. Reseal the shaker and shake vigorously without ice until completely emulsified, about 15 seconds. Double-strain into a chilled coupe or Nick and Nora glass. Express lime twist over the top and discard. Garnish with nutmeg.

BLACKBERRY-CUCUMBER MULE

MAKES 1 DRINK

Just when this crowd-pleasing berry drink from Michael Neff of The Three Clubs in Los Angeles heats things up—hi there, ginger beer—it starts to cool things down, thanks to muddled cucumber and mint. The contrast comes out in every sip. I find myself quickly taking another sip and meeting the bottom of the glass way too soon. Feel more like gin tonight? This drink will happily swing that way too.

3 ripe blackberries

2 cucumber slices, ¼ inch thick

10 fresh mint leaves

2 ounces vodka

¾ ounce fresh lemon juice

½ ounce 1:1 simple syrup (page 13)

2½ ounces ginger beer

GARNISH: mint sprig and cucumber wheel

Muddle blackberries, cucumber, and mint in the smaller half of a cocktail shaker. Add vodka, lemon juice, and simple syrup and fill with ice. Shake until well chilled, about 12 seconds. Double-strain into an ice-filled collins glass, pour the ginger beer down the side of the glass, and give it a brief, gentle stir. Garnish with mint sprig and cucumber wheel, plus a straw if you have one.

BO NuS DRINKS

Try substituting vodka for the spirit in the drinks below.

SLIPPERY WHEN WET

MAKES 1 DRINK

I adore this fragrant and refreshing strawberry-gin drink, created by Shannon Tebay Sidle of New York's Slowly Shirley and Death & Co. The secret ingredient is a dollop of unsweetened Greek yogurt, which gives the cocktail a tangy flavor and subtly creamy texture. The final result isn't sweet or smoothie-like; this is definitely still a cocktail. A sprinkle of freshly ground black pepper highlights the gin's herbal character, but I also like this drink with grassy blanco tequila or a full-bodied aged rum. If your fridge doesn't dispense crushed ice, fill a freezer bag with cubes, wrap them in a dish towel, and go wild with a meat tenderizer or rolling pin.

1 large or 2 small ripe strawberries, halved

¾ ounce fresh lemon juice

½ ounce undiluted honey

2 ounces gin

1 heaping teaspoon plain Greek yogurt

GARNISH: freshly ground black pepper and a vertical slice of strawberry

Combine strawberries, lemon juice, and honey in a cocktail shaker and muddle until well broken up. Add gin and Greek yogurt and fill shaker with ice. Shake until well chilled, about 15 seconds. Fill a rocks glass with crushed ice, then double-strain cocktail into it. Grind black pepper on top and garnish with the strawberry slice.

3 BEET HIGH AND RISING

MAKES 1 DRINK

I love fancy Italian vermouths like Carpano Antica Formula for the velvety texture and complex flavor they add to cocktails. But this drink offers similar rich bass notes and a touch of earthy sweetness thanks to an unexpected combination—beet juice and a few drops of vanilla extract. Created by Chris Morris of Ready Room in Houston, this fizzy, shaken aperitif doesn't end up tasting vegetal or particularly savory. Instead, the beets deepen the berry flavor (and hue) of the mix of pomegranate soda, lemon juice, and gin. You certainly can juice your own beets for this, but it also works wonderfully with a high-quality bottled juice like Love Beets. Since it's not served over ice, it's really worth chilling the glass to help this drink stay cool.

1½ ounces gin

2 drops vanilla extract (be careful, don't add more!)

¾ ounce 1:1 simple syrup (page 13)

½ ounce beet juice

½ ounce fresh lemon juice

1 egg white or ¾ ounce aquafaba (see page 17)

2½ ounces chilled pomegranate soda (such as Izze)

Combine gin, vanilla, simple syrup, beet juice, lemon juice, and egg white in a cocktail shaker and shake without ice until emulsified, about 10 seconds. Add ice, reseal the shaker, and shake vigorously until well chilled and very frothy, about 30 seconds—it's longer than you'd think. Double-strain into a chilled 12-ounce collins glass. Let foam settle, then slowly top off with pomegranate soda until the foam rises above the rim of the glass.

JE NE SAIS QUOI

MAKES 1 DRINK

Anise flavors are a hallmark of today's cocktails, often added to a drink through a splash of absinthe or Chartreuse. But tarragon gives you a lovely anise note without the extra $40 bottle. The soft licorice flavor of the fresh herb mingles beautifully here with tart green grapes (or adorable teeny champagne grapes, if you can find them). Bethany Kocak of Animal in Los Angeles pairs the elegant combination with juniper-laced gin and softens the mix with a frothy egg white.

Small handful champagne grapes or 5 tart green seedless grapes

Leaves from 3 tarragon sprigs

½ ounce 1:1 simple syrup (page 13)

1½ ounces gin

¾ ounce fresh lime juice

1 egg white or ¾ ounce aquafaba (see page 17)

Combine grapes, tarragon leaves, and simple syrup in a shaker and muddle just until juice has been released from the grapes. Add gin, lime juice, and egg white and shake without ice until emulsified, about 20 seconds. Add ice, reseal shaker, and shake vigorously until well chilled and very frothy, about 30 seconds. Double-strain into a chilled coupe glass.

THE
GINCIDENT

MAKES 1 DRINK

Blueberries can be a little weak in cocktails; the old muddle-and-smash routine doesn't impart much berry character. But heating the berries briefly until they pop concentrates their flavor, and this drink, adapted from Kristina Magro of Pub Royale and Estereo in Chicago, is bold, tart, and refreshing. She accentuates the foresty flavors of gin with rosemary and basil; a bunch of extra leaves used as a garnish will boost the aroma further. This drink is also great with vodka or tequila. I'll leave it to you to dream up a name for your favorite version.

2 ounces gin

1 ounce blueberry syrup (see recipe)

1 ounce fresh lemon juice

2 large fresh basil leaves, torn

5 fresh rosemary leaves, torn

GARNISH: basil sprig

Combine gin, blueberry syrup, lemon juice, basil, and rosemary in a cocktail shaker and fill with ice. Shake until well chilled, about 12 seconds. Double-strain into an ice-filled rocks glass, garnishing with a basil sprig.

BLUEBERRY SYRUP
MAKES ABOUT 13 OUNCES, ENOUGH FOR 13 DRINKS

1 cup water

1 cup sugar

1 heaping cup ripe blueberries

Combine water, sugar, and blueberries in a saucepan and warm over medium-high heat, stirring until sugar dissolves. Cook just until berries begin to pop, about 8 minutes; be sure to remove from the heat before the syrup reaches a rapid boil so that it doesn't become jammy. Smash berries with the back of a spoon, then let cool. Strain through a fine-mesh strainer set over a resealable container, pressing on solids to extract juice. Refrigerate for up to 3 days.

POROM

MAKES 1 DRINK

There's a reason the Paloma, a simple mix of grapefruit soda and tequila, is beloved. The pithy, bittersweet flavor of the fruit is the ideal backdrop for the grassy notes of that spirit. But in some ways, herbal tequila and botanical gin are cousins, and it's the juniper-laced gin that I prefer in this grapefruity drink from Tom Lindstedt of Portland's Barlow Artisanal Bar. The tangy citrus soda is amplified with two ounces of fresh fruit juice, and muddled aromatic fennel boosts the drink's smooth and cooling herbal side. (That's not to say you shouldn't try it with blanco tequila, though; that version's pretty darn tasty too.)

⅓ fennel bulb, thinly sliced

1½ ounces gin

1 ounce fresh tangerine or orange juice

1 ounce fresh grapefruit juice

1½ ounces chilled grapefruit soda (such as San Pellegrino Pompelmo or Izze)

GARNISH: fennel frond and freshly grated nutmeg

Combine fennel and gin in a cocktail shaker and muddle until broken up, about 20 seconds. Add tangerine and grapefruit juices and fill with ice. Shake until well chilled, about 12 seconds. Double-strain into an ice-filled collins glass, top off with measured grapefruit soda, and give it a brief, gentle stir. Garnish with fennel frond and freshly grated nutmeg.

GORILLA MONSOON

MAKES 1 DRINK

I rarely feel inspired by a riff on the gin and tonic, but this drink is really something special. Mango chutney is a powerhouse that balances richly perfumed fruit with ginger, vinegar, and spices. (Look for one without too many ingredients and opt out of versions with garlic early in the list.) Here, Brian Griffiths of Over Under in Miami pairs the sweet-and-savory preserves with garam masala, a spice blend that includes coriander, cloves, cinnamon, cumin, and cardamom. To avoid a gritty mess of ground spices, you'll warm the spice mix in water, then strain it out with a coffee filter. The extra attention to detail is worth it.

1½ ounces gin

¾ ounce fresh lime juice

½ ounce garam masala syrup (see recipe)

1 teaspoon mango chutney (such as Sukhi's)

1½ ounces chilled tonic water (such as Fever-Tree)

GARNISH: lime twist and a straw

Combine gin, lime juice, garam masala syrup, and mango chutney in a cocktail shaker and fill with ice. Shake until well chilled, about 12 seconds. Unseal shaker and add tonic water, then strain into an ice-filled collins glass. Garnish with a lime twist and serve with a straw.

GARAM MASALA SYRUP

MAKES 14 OUNCES, ENOUGH FOR 28 DRINKS

1 tablespoon ground garam masala

1 cup water

1½ cups sugar

Combine garam masala and water in a small saucepan and bring to a boil over medium-high heat, watching carefully. Immediately remove from heat and strain through a coffee filter set over a clean resealable container with a tight-fitting lid. Add sugar to the strained liquid and stir or shake until dissolved. Refrigerate for up to 2 weeks.

GIN ROCKET

MAKES 1 DRINK

Portland- and San Francisco–based bartender Kate Bolton has the touch for subtle, delicate drinks that go wonderfully with food. This spin on the gimlet is no exception: shaking shaved fennel and muddled arugula into the drink gives it an anise-and-pepper flavor that's ideal for serving with seafood or light pasta dishes.

1 fennel bulb with fronds

¼ cup packed arugula leaves

¾ ounce fresh lime juice

¾ ounce 1:1 simple syrup (page 13)

2 ounces gin

GARNISH: lime wheel, arugula leaf, or peppery flower (such as nasturtium; optional)

Using a mandoline or vegetable peeler, thinly slice enough of the fennel bulb to yield ¼ cup (about ½ small bulb). Add a pinch of the fennel fronds to a cocktail shaker along with sliced fennel and arugula leaves. Add lime juice and simple syrup and muddle until the fennel is bruised. Add gin and fill with ice. Shake vigorously until chilled, about 12 seconds. Double-strain into a chilled coupe glass and garnish with lime wheel, arugula leaf, or nasturtium if desired.

POLICE AND THIEVES

MAKES 1 DRINK

Frank Cisneros says this is probably the most popular cocktail he's ever made; it was on the menu at Gin Palace in New York's East Village for years. Upon first taste, you'll see why it was such a crowd-pleaser. It's a sunny, warming drink, thanks to pineapple's heady tropical flavor and a spicy cinnamon simple syrup, all perked up with grapefruit, lime, and piney gin.

There's no need to get out a juicer for this; just muddle a 2- to 3-inch chunk of fresh pineapple and strain through a fine-mesh strainer into your measuring cup or jigger. This drink would be totally at home at a tiki party; you can multiply the recipe (and make fresh pineapple juice by whirring chopped fruit in your blender, then straining), but don't try to shake more than two drinks at a time.

2 ounces gin

½ ounce cinnamon syrup (see recipe)

½ ounce fresh pineapple juice

½ ounce fresh lime juice

¼ ounce fresh grapefruit juice

Combine gin, cinnamon syrup, pineapple juice, lime juice, and grapefruit juice in a cocktail shaker and fill with ice. Shake until well chilled, about 12 seconds. Double-strain into a chilled coupe glass.

CINNAMON SYRUP
MAKES ABOUT 12 OUNCES, ENOUGH FOR 24 DRINKS

1 cup water
1 cup sugar
5 cinnamon sticks

Combine water and sugar in a small saucepan and warm over medium heat, stirring until sugar is dissolved. Break up cinnamon sticks and add to the syrup, then increase heat to medium-high and bring to a boil, stirring occasionally. Remove from heat and let sit, covered, for 1 to 2 hours. Strain through a fine-mesh strainer set over a resealable container. Refrigerate for up to 1 week.

BAY OF BENGAL

MAKES 1 DRINK

Coconut and gin have a strange but undeniable affinity: the richness of the former craves the freshness of the latter. And while time-intensive infusions and syrups are often required to give a drink some spice, this concoction from Collin Nicholas of Bellota in San Francisco gets its alluringly complex flavor profile from the simple addition of ground curry powder, a packaged blend that often includes warming spices like turmeric, cumin, cinnamon, and ginger. All you have to do is spoon the spice mix in and shake well to get a little foam going, then serve over a big ice cube. This drink is also fantastic with floral pisco or herb-tinged blanco tequila. Note that you shouldn't be using sweetened Coco López or regular coconut milk here. Look for thick, rich, unsweetened coconut *cream* in the Asian foods aisle of your supermarket; it's available in both canned and boxed versions.

1 ½ ounces gin

½ ounce 3:1 agave syrup (page 14)

½ ounce fresh lemon juice

½ ounce unsweetened coconut cream

½ ounce rice milk (such as Rice Dream Original)

1 egg white or ¾ ounce aquafaba (see page 17)

½ teaspoon curry powder

GARNISH: lemon twist

Combine gin, agave syrup, lemon juice, coconut cream, rice milk, egg white, and curry powder in a cocktail shaker and shake without ice until emulsified, about 20 seconds. Add ice, reseal the shaker, and shake vigorously for 20 full seconds—put some muscle into it. Strain into a large rocks glass over a big ice cube and garnish with lemon twist.

ROSE OF ALL ROSES

MAKES 1 DRINK

Delicately floral and cucumbery gin drinks are always pretty delightful, especially during brunch, but this one from Elsa Taylor of The Roost on Corydon in Winnipeg gets extra points for presentation: you'll decorate the tall glass by alternating ice and cucumber slices from bottom to top of each collins glass. White tea and rose water (which is available in the baking or Middle Eastern section of your grocery store) give the drink subtle perfume without going overboard. A platter of crustless sandwiches wouldn't be out of place as an accompaniment—this is elegant stuff.

8 to 10 thin cucumber wheels

2 ounces gin

1½ ounces brewed white tea, cooled

½ ounce fresh lemon juice

½ ounce 1:1 simple syrup (page 13)

2 drops rose water (be careful, don't add more!)

Pinch salt

½ ounce chilled club soda

GARNISH:
pinch salt and mint sprig

Combine 2 of the cucumber wheels, gin, white tea, lemon juice, simple syrup, rose water, and salt in a cocktail shaker.

Prepare a collins glass by layering ice cubes and the remaining cucumber slices, alternating back and forth until the glass is three-quarters full.

Fill cocktail shaker with ice and shake vigorously until well chilled, about 15 seconds. Unseal shaker and add club soda. Strain into prepared glass. Garnish with a small pinch of salt and a mint sprig.

THE BANGKOK

MAKES 1 DRINK

Connoisseurs of spicy Thai food will appreciate this mint-laced drink, which is spiked with muddled sweet-hot red Fresno chile. Smashed lemongrass offers a softly vegetal, citrusy flavor that boosts the botanical side of London dry gin. Christopher Longoria of 1760 in San Francisco came up with the drink while on a trip to the Thai capital. Warning: If you're sensitive to spice, you may want to consider dialing down the chile here.

3 ½-inch piece lemongrass

¾ ounce fresh lemon juice

1 or 2 very thin slices Fresno chile

2 teaspoons superfine sugar

25 fresh mint leaves

1 ½ ounces gin

2 ounces chilled club soda

GARNISH: mint sprig and lemongrass, sliced into long, slim strips (optional)

Remove tough outer layer from lemongrass and chop into short segments. Muddle lemongrass with lemon juice, chile, and superfine sugar in a cocktail shaker until lemongrass is well bruised. Add mint and muddle gently a few more times. Add gin and fill cocktail shaker with ice. Shake until well chilled, about 20 seconds. Double-strain into an ice-filled collins glass, pour the measured club soda down the side of the glass, and give it a brief, gentle stir. Garnish with mint sprig and lemongrass strips, if desired.

THE NIGHT
OF THE HUNTER

MAKES 1 DRINK

I'm not sure how she does it, but with this drink, gin maven Keli Rivers of Whitechapel in San Francisco conjures tropical flavors from a handful of plump figs, a few sprigs of thyme, and some pink grapefruit soda. Since fig seeds gather in the strainer, it takes an extra moment to strain the muddled mixture, but your patience will be rewarded.

3 ripe figs, halved

2 ounces gin

1¼ ounces fresh lemon juice

¾ ounce 1:1 simple syrup (page 13)

Leaves from 3 thyme sprigs

2½ ounces chilled grapefruit soda (such as Izze)

GARNISH: lemon wheel and thyme sprig

Muddle figs in the smaller half of a cocktail shaker until well broken up. Add gin, lemon juice, simple syrup, and thyme leaves and fill with ice. Shake until well chilled, about 12 seconds. Double-strain into an ice-filled rocks glass, stirring the solids in the strainer as needed to let the liquid through. Pour the grapefruit soda down the side of the glass, and give it a brief, gentle stir. Garnish with lemon wheel and thyme sprig.

BO NuS DRINKS

Try substituting gin for the spirit in the drinks below.

BOOGIE NIGHTS

MAKES 1 DRINK

The pollen gathered from fennel plants is amazingly aromatic and adds a wonderfully fresh anise flavor wherever it's used. It's more and more widely available these days and handy to have around for rubbing on a pork roast or sprinkling onto pasta. Get some and try it in this vibrant, juicy, but not-too-sweet cocktail from Andrew Moore of Ox in Portland. The fennel pollen brings out the hidden floral notes in ripe strawberries while emphasizing the layered, herbal complexity of silver tequila. Can't find fennel pollen? You can also make this drink with ground fennel seeds.

1¼ ounces fresh lime juice, divided

1 teaspoon plus 3 pinches fennel pollen or ground fennel seeds, divided

½ teaspoon kosher salt

3 ripe strawberries

2 ounces blanco tequila

½ ounce 2:1 agave syrup (page 14)

GARNISH: fennel frond (optional)

To rim the glass, pour ½ ounce of the lime juice onto a small plate. Stir together 1 teaspoon of the fennel pollen and salt on another small plate. Dip a rocks glass first into the lime juice, then dip and roll it into the fennel salt mixture. Set aside.

Muddle strawberries with the remaining 3 pinches fennel pollen in a cocktail shaker until well broken up. Add tequila, remaining ¾ ounce lime juice, and agave syrup and fill with ice. Shake until well chilled, about 15 seconds. Fill the rimmed glass with ice and double-strain the cocktail into it. Garnish with fennel frond if desired.

SUN-KISSED HIGHBALL

MAKES 1 DRINK

I love that this easy highball brings together two succulents. The agave that tequila is made from isn't actually that closely related to spiky aloe, but the two plants look strikingly similar and also taste great together. This drink is softly herbal and tart, served tall in a skinny collins glass. It's the ideal option for your friend who says, "Cocktails are always too sweet."

Sother Teague, beverage director of New York's Amor y Amargo, designed this recipe to be flexible: if you don't have tequila on hand, try subbing in gin or light rum. The final flavor will also vary depending on which aloe juice you buy. I recommend the widely available Alo Exposed brand, which is sweetened with honey.

2 ounces aloe vera juice
(such as Alo Exposed)

2 ounces blanco tequila

¾ ounce fresh lime juice

1¾ ounces chilled club soda

Pour aloe vera juice and tequila into a collins glass. Add lime juice and carefully drop the spent lime rind into your glass. Stir together to mix, top with club soda and ice, and give it another gentle stir.

SUCIA REINA

MAKES 1 DRINK

This drink, whose Spanish name translates to "dirty queen," isn't all-out savory, though a little olive brine and a garnish of mild green Castelvetrano olives brings out the mouthwatering, slightly salty side of blanco tequila. In this recipe, created by Karen Fu of Donna Cocktail Club in Brooklyn, the drink's citrus backbone is shored up with fresh juice, bittersweet marmalade, and a single ounce of sweet soda. Altogether, it's balanced and just a little out of the ordinary.

1½ ounces blanco tequila

½ ounce olive brine from Castelvetrano or California ripe black olives

½ ounce fresh lemon juice

½ ounce fresh orange juice

¼ ounce undiluted agave nectar

1 heaping teaspoon orange marmalade (such as Bonne Maman)

1 ounce chilled lemon-lime soda (such as Maine Root)

GARNISH: orange wedge and 3 Castelvetrano olives

Combine tequila, olive brine, lemon juice, orange juice, agave nectar, and marmalade in a cocktail shaker and fill with ice. Shake until well chilled, about 12 seconds. Unseal shaker and add lemon-lime soda. Strain into an ice-filled collins glass. Garnish with orange wedge and olives.

GREEN GOLD

MAKES 1 DRINK

Combining pineapple, lime, and tequila may sound like a throwback to the fruity cocktails of decades past, but this drink has a punch of the unexpected: a gutsy but well-rounded green pepper flavor that's a mix of muddled bell pepper and buzzy jalapeño. Birmingham-based bartender Laura Newman makes this with two slices of jalapeño per drink, but I'd recommend starting with one unless you're a certified capsaicin fanatic. Fresh pineapple keeps things bright and balanced; don't substitute tinny shelf-stable juice. All you need to do is muddle a 2- to 3-inch chunk of fresh pineapple and strain the juice through a fine-mesh strainer before you measure.

¼ ounce plus 1 teaspoon agave nectar

¼ ounce hot water

3 (1-inch) square pieces green bell pepper

1 or 2 thin slices jalapeño chile

2 ounces blanco tequila

¾ ounce fresh lime juice

½ ounce fresh pineapple juice

GARNISH: pineapple triangle and jalapeño slice on a cocktail pick

In a cocktail shaker, stir together agave nectar and water to loosen, then let cool. Add bell pepper and jalapeño and muddle until bruised. (You're not creating a puree; just bash it enough to crack them open a bit.) Add tequila, lime juice, and pineapple juice and fill the cocktail shaker with ice. Shake until well chilled, about 20 seconds. Double-strain into an ice-filled rocks glass. Garnish with speared pineapple and jalapeño.

TAMARINDO AGUAS FRESCAS

MAKES 8 DRINKS

The best cocktails have a bit of mystery, with layers of flavors that unfold and keep you guessing. This big-batch drink from Ben Potts of Beaker and Gray in Miami has a tangy, citrusy flavor that's underscored by a deep richness, thanks to a little tamarind concentrate. Complex in flavor doesn't mean complex to make: this drink sets off sparks even though you simply pour sweet tangerine and fresh lime juice into a pitcher with the tamarind concentrate, tequila, a little water, and simple syrup. It's especially refreshing when served over crushed ice. Feel free to double or triple the recipe for a thirsty crowd.

12 ¾ ounces boiling water

3 ½ ounces tamarind concentrate (such as Tamicon)

10 ounces 1:1 simple syrup (page 13)

8 ½ ounces reposado tequila

8 ½ ounces fresh tangerine or mandarin orange juice

8 ½ ounces fresh lime juice

GARNISH:
12 lime or tangerine wheels

In a 2-quart pitcher or resealable container, stir together the boiling water and tamarind concentrate to loosen until the tamarind is dissolved. Stir in simple syrup and let cool. Add tequila, tangerine juice, and lime juice, and stir well to mix. Refrigerate for at least 30 minutes and up to 6 hours. When ready to serve, fill collins or rocks glasses with crushed ice and pour cocktail into them, garnishing pitcher and glasses with lime or tangerine wheels.

OLIVIA FLIP

MAKES 1 DRINK

Nicholas Bennett of Porchlight in New York dreamed up this remarkable drink, which draws out the floral, peppery character of aged tequila by pairing the spirit with a little good olive oil. While the drink also includes a whole egg, which helps the flavorful oil to emulsify properly, this is nothing like heavy eggnog. Instead, it's remarkably light and subtle on the palate. As far as the oil goes, it's worth it to use your best. As Bennett notes, "You're going to be drinking it, not cooking in spices or garlic and onions. Invest in something nice!" Instead of bland refined sugar, use demerara or turbinado (such as Sugar in the Raw) for extra body and flavor.

2 ounces reposado tequila

¾ ounce fresh lemon juice

½ ounce 1:1 simple syrup made with demerara or turbinado sugar (page 13)

½ ounce high-quality extra-virgin olive oil

Pinch sea salt

1 egg

GARNISH: star anise pod

Combine tequila, lemon juice, simple syrup, olive oil, salt, and egg in a cocktail shaker and shake vigorously without ice until emulsified, about 20 seconds. Fill shaker with ice, reseal, and shake vigorously until well chilled and very frothy, about 30 seconds. Double-strain into a chilled wine glass. Garnish with star anise.

TIBURON

MAKES 1 DRINK

If you love margaritas but don't have triple sec or another orange liqueur on hand, never fear: this tasty, honey-sweetened drink from T. Cole Newton of Twelve Mile Limit in New Orleans will do the trick. Salt the rim and use good honey; it adds a touch of floral richness that shines in the simple combination. Chile-heads might be tempted to dump in more Tabasco, but I urge you not to: made with a single dash, the drink is perfectly balanced, with a touch of umami and warmth. Much more, and you've got vinegar taking center stage.

1 lime wedge

Kosher salt

1½ ounces reposado tequila

½ ounce fresh lime juice

¾ ounce 2:1 honey syrup (page 14)

Dash Tabasco

Wet the rim of a rocks glass with a lime wedge, then dip or roll the glass in a small plate of kosher salt.

Combine tequila, lime juice, honey syrup, and Tabasco in a cocktail shaker and fill with ice. Shake until well chilled, about 12 seconds. Fill the rimmed glass with ice and strain cocktail into It.

LA VERDUDERIA

MAKES 1 DRINK

This tangy and slightly spicy drink, sweetened with Jarritos mango soda, pays tribute to the Mexican grocery store, a treasure trove of tasty stuff for putting in cocktails. A little cilantro adds a subtle green flavor that balances the drink's fruity side. Bartender Pilar Vree, who has worked at Sidebar and Penrose in Oakland, rims the glass with Tajín, a Mexican seasoning mix that includes chiles, lime juice, and salt. If you can't find the hot-tart spice mix, you can garnish your glass with a blend of cayenne or paprika and kosher salt. Vree recommends pairing this drink with a snack of chicharrones and spiced peanuts for the full experience.

1 teaspoon Tajín seasoning

1 ounce fresh lime juice, divided

2 ounces reposado tequila

½ ounce fresh grapefruit juice

3 cilantro sprigs

2 dashes Cholula or other hot sauce

1¾ ounces chilled mango soda (such as Jarritos)

GARNISH: candied mango slice on a cocktail pick, with lime wheel and pickled jalapeño chile slice (optional)

To rim the glass, pour Tajín seasoning onto a small plate and ½ ounce of the lime juice onto another plate. Dip a collins glass first into the lime juice, then dip and roll it into the Tajín. Set aside.

Combine tequila, grapefruit juice, remaining ½ ounce lime juice, cilantro, and hot sauce in a cocktail shaker and fill with ice. Shake until well chilled, about 12 seconds. Unseal shaker and add mango soda. Fill rimmed glass with ice and strain cocktail into it. Garnish with a speared candied mango, plus pickled jalapeño and lime wheel if desired.

TATTLETALE

MAKES 1 DRINK

Leave it to Heather Sang and Benjamin Amberg of Portland's Clyde Common to offer a tart and lightly spiced cocktail that's redolent of sour green apples and cream, enriched with grassy aged tequila and, uh-huh, marshmallow creme. "I liked the idea of using junk to make something really good," Amberg says. The white stuff gives this drink a delicate vanilla flavor and luxurious texture, plus a touch of foam on top of every sip.

1½ ounces reposado tequila

¾ ounce fresh lime juice

¾ ounce marshmallow creme

2 teaspoons apple butter

Combine all the ingredients in the larger half of a cocktail shaker and blend with an immersion blender to incorporate the marshmallow creme. Fill the cocktail shaker with ice and shake vigorously until well chilled, about 15 seconds. Double-strain into a chilled coupe glass.

FRENCH CONCESSION

MAKES 1 DRINK

Cinnamon, spice, and whiskey are nice, but this drink proves that autumnal flavors like crisp apples and the ginger, cloves, cinnamon, anise seed, and star anise that make up Chinese five-spice powder are also well paired with spicy reposado tequila. This boldly flavored make-at-home recipe created by Christopher Lowder, head bartender at Proof & Company in Shanghai, has you shake the five-spice right in with the spirit, along with honey, fresh lemon, and apple juice.

It makes a huge difference to use tangy, freshly pressed Granny Smith apple juice instead of flatter-tasting bottled juice. Promise me you'll try it with the fresh stuff if you have access to a juicer (or a food processor and strainer). If you don't have a way to make fresh juice, use unfiltered apple cider or cold-pressed apple juice from a farmers' market vendor or the refrigerated section of your grocery store. Just be mindful that you may need an extra teaspoon of lemon juice and a touch more honey to make it sing.

1½ ounces reposado tequila

1½ ounces fresh Granny Smith apple juice

½ ounce 2:1 honey syrup (page 14)

½ ounce fresh lemon juice

Generous ¼ teaspoon five-spice powder

GARNISH: star anise pod (optional)

Combine tequila, apple juice, honey syrup, lemon juice, and five-spice powder in a cocktail shaker and fill with ice. Shake until well chilled, about 15 seconds. Strain into a chilled coupe or Nick and Nora glass. Garnish with star anise, if desired.

GRILLED MARGARITA

MAKES 2 DRINKS

In simple recipes, the little things count. This margarita variation, sent my way by Kamil Foltan when he was at the Potato Head Beach Club in Bali, Indonesia, gets a caramelly richness from aged tequila and agave nectar, bumped up with grilled lemon halves. If you've never thrown citrus on the grill or into a skillet before, you're in for a treat: the fruit gets browned quickly, then adds a slightly sweet, toasty flavor to the drink. Use the best tequila you have on hand, or try it with mezcal, light rum, or bourbon. I like to add a pinch of salt on top.

2 large or 3 small lemons, plus 2 lemon wheels

4 ounces reposado or añejo tequila

1¼ ounces 2:1 honey syrup (page 14)

GARNISH: 2 rosemary sprigs and 2 pinches flaky salt (optional)

Preheat a grill to medium-high or warm a skillet over medium-high heat. Cut whole lemons in half and place cut sides down on the hot grill or skillet. Add lemon wheels to grill or skillet. Cook until lemon flesh is browned, about 4 to 6 minutes. (There's no need to cook both sides of the wheels.) Remove from heat and let cool to room temperature. Set aside lemon wheels for garnish. Juice lemon halves and measure out 2 ounces grilled lemon juice. (Use any extra in salad dressing!)

Combine measured lemon juice, tequila, and honey syrup in a cocktail shaker and fill with ice. Shake until well chilled, about 15 seconds. Strain into 2 chilled coupe glasses or ice-filled rocks glasses. Garnish with grilled lemon wheels (charred side up), rosemary sprig, and a pinch of flaky salt if desired.

SASSY FLOWER

MAKES 1 DRINK

Alan Ruesga-Pelayo of Cosme in New York grew up in Mexico enjoying his mother's and grandmother's homemade aguas frescas. His favorite was always the hibiscus-flavored version, *agua de jamaica*, which inspired this drink. Tangy hibiscus tea is steeped with fresh rosemary, giving you a piney flavor that draws out the woodsy side of mezcal. If you prep the syrup early and stash it in your fridge, finishing the drink is a snap.

2 ounces mezcal

1 ounce fresh lemon juice

¾ ounce hibiscus-rosemary syrup (see recipe)

GARNISH: rosemary sprig

Combine mezcal, lemon juice, and hibiscus-rosemary syrup in a cocktail shaker and fill with ice. Shake until well chilled, about 12 seconds. Strain into an ice-filled rocks glass and garnish with a rosemary sprig.

HIBISCUS-ROSEMARY SYRUP
MAKES ABOUT 14 OUNCES, ENOUGH FOR 18 DRINKS

2 hibiscus tea bags (such as Traditional Medicinals)
1 rosemary sprig
1 cup boiling water
1½ cups sugar

Steep tea bags and rosemary in boiling water for 5 minutes. Strain into a resealable container with a tight-fitting lid, then add sugar and stir or shake until dissolved. Let cool, then refrigerate for up to 2 weeks.

DOMO ARIGATO

MAKES 1 DRINK

It may sound really out-there to use sesame oil in a cocktail, but this fantastic drink, created by Ran Duan of the Baldwin Bar at Sichuan Garden in Woburn, Massachusetts, is delicately spicy, tart, and just subtly savory. If you've never made cocktails with mezcal, this is a great place to start. It's become my dinner party favorite.

Just be sure to use fresh ginger juice, since sugary ginger syrup or acrid bottled juice will throw the drink out of whack. If you don't have a juicer or a friendly local juice shop, you can muddle some chopped ginger or grate it with a Microplane, then press it against a fine-mesh strainer to get the liquid out, or grind your peeled, sliced ginger in a blender or food processor before straining. If you're making the drink for guests, prep the ginger juice up to 1 hour in advance and store in your fridge.

2 ounces mezcal

1 ounce 1:1 simple syrup (page 13)

¾ ounce fresh lime juice

¼ ounce plus 1 teaspoon fresh ginger juice

2 drops toasted sesame oil

1½ ounces chilled club soda

Combine mezcal, simple syrup, lime juice, ginger juice, and sesame oil in a cocktail shaker and fill with ice. Shake until well chilled, about 15 seconds. Unseal shaker and add club soda. Strain into an ice-filled collins glass.

HEART OF FIRE

MAKES 1 DRINK

This tall, hot-and-cooling drink was created by Chelan Finney, who has graced such bars as Del Posto and the John Dory Oyster Bar in New York, as well as Ounce Taipei. It's especially gorgeous when made with bold red blood orange to match the blood orange soda (San Pellegrino Aranciata Rossa is perfect; the Trader Joe's brand works, too). But don't let a lack of blood oranges stop you from making this cocktail. It's still plenty delicious with whatever fresh oranges you have on hand. Muddling the orange slices brings out the fragrant, slightly bitter oils from the peel. The core of this drink, though, is the mezcal, which offers a hint of bacon that cozies up to the honey and spicy jalapeño (use just one slice if you're heat-averse). Brunch will never be the same.

2 slices blood orange or navel orange, peel on

1 or 2 very thin slices jalapeño chile

1½ ounces mezcal

¾ ounce fresh lime juice

½ ounce undiluted honey

3 ounces blood orange soda (such as San Pellegrino Aranciata Rossa or Trader Joe's)

GARNISH:
orange wheel (optional)

Muddle orange slices and jalapeño in the smaller half of a cocktail shaker just until jalapeño is broken up. Don't pulverize the orange slices. In the larger half of a cocktail shaker, stir together mezcal, lime juice, and honey. Pour mezcal mix into the shaker with the muddled ingredients, fill with ice, and shake until well chilled, about 15 seconds. Unseal shaker and add blood orange soda. Strain into an ice-filled collins glass. Garnish with an orange wheel if desired.

MARRAKESH EXPRESS

MAKES 1 DRINK

You can buy 100 percent pomegranate juice at many grocery stores, but the fresh stuff is even better: it's both brighter and more intense in flavor. It's also remarkably easy to get at—you can put chunky quarters or sixths of a whole pomegranate in your manual citrus squeezer and press the juice right out, no seed-gathering required. It takes just a minute or two to get enough for this impressively complex and elegant mezcal cocktail created by Gabriella Mlynarczyk of Birch in Los Angeles. The fresh pomegranate juice truly shines, with a backdrop of savory harissa heat and a balanced floral aroma from rose water and lemon. A splash of aquafaba adds a delicately foamy texture while keeping the drink vegan-friendly; egg white is a fine substitute if you don't have chickpeas around.

1½ ounces mezcal

1½ ounces pomegranate juice (fresh preferred)

¾ ounce lemon juice

¾ ounce 1:1 simple syrup (page 13)

½ to 1 teaspoon harissa paste (such as Dea), depending on how spicy you want it

¾ teaspoon rose water

Splash aquafaba (see page 17) or egg white

GARNISH: pinch each pomegranate seeds, cracked pink peppercorns, and flaky salt (black, smoked, or Maldon)

Combine mezcal, pomegranate juice, lemon juice, simple syrup, harissa, rose water, and aquafaba in a cocktail shaker and shake vigorously without ice for 20 seconds to emulsify. Add ice, reseal shaker, and shake until chilled and foamy, about 30 seconds. Strain into an ice-filled rocks glass. Garnish with a sprinkle of pomegranate seeds, cracked pink peppercorns, and flaky salt.

DESERT SUNSET

MAKES 1 DRINK

Carrot cocktails sometimes end up tasting oddly healthy. But this one from Chad Hauge of Chicago's Longman & Eagle is just pure fun. It's salty, bright, smoky, and fresh—the kind of thing that'll get you dancing. Orange and lime juices give the carrot juice a lift, and leathery mezcal finds its match in a rim of salt and smoked paprika. If you don't have a bottle of mezcal, you should get some. Liquor store's closed? Blanco tequila will do.

1¼ ounces fresh lime juice, divided

2 teaspoons coarse salt

½ teaspoon smoked hot paprika

2 ounces mezcal

½ ounce 1:1 agave syrup (page 14)

1 ounce fresh carrot juice

½ ounce fresh orange juice

To rim the glass, pour ½ ounce of the lime juice onto a small plate. Stir together salt and smoked hot paprika on another small plate. Dip a rocks glass first into the lime juice, then dip and roll it in the paprika mixture. Set aside.

Combine mezcal, agave syrup, carrot juice, orange juice, and remaining ¾ ounce lime juice in a cocktail shaker and fill with ice. Shake vigorously until well chilled, about 12 seconds. Fill the rimmed glass with ice and double-strain the cocktail into it.

DR. GREEN THUMB

MAKES 1 DRINK

Celery can sometimes be too aggressive, taking over a cocktail with its pungent vegetal flavor. But in this delicate, fizzy drink from Tommy Quimby of Rich Table in San Francisco, the celery is tempered with frothy egg white and a light pour of mezcal, which adds a flavor reminiscent of good olive oil. This is the perfect cocktail to serve with ceviche, lobster rolls, or summer salads. If you don't have a juicer (or a friendly juice bar nearby), whir some celery in a blender and then strain to get at the juice.

1 ¼ ounces mezcal
1 ounce fresh celery juice
½ ounce fresh lime juice
½ ounce 1:1 simple syrup
(page 13)
1 egg white
1 ounce chilled seltzer

GARNISH:
pinch ground celery seeds
and a straw (optional)

Combine mezcal, celery juice, lime juice, simple syrup, and egg white in a cocktail shaker and shake without ice until emulsified, about 10 seconds. Unseal shaker, add ice, and shake vigorously for 30 seconds more until well chilled and very frothy. Strain into an empty chilled collins glass and top with seltzer. Garnish with ground celery seeds and serve with a straw if desired.

BO NuS DRINKS

Try substituting agave spirits in the drinks below.

More drinks to make with blanco tequila:

SLIPPERY WHEN WET (page 38) *Strawberry • lemon • Greek yogurt • black pepper*

JE NE SAIS QUOI (page 42) *Green grapes • tarragon*

THE GINCIDENT (page 45) *Blueberries • basil • rosemary • lemon*

POLICE AND THIEVES (page 51) *Pineapple • grapefruit • cinnamon*

BAY OF BENGAL (page 52) *Coconut • rice milk • curry powder*

SASSY FLOWER (page 81) *Hibiscus • rosemary • lemon*

DESERT SUNSET (page 89) *Carrot • orange • lime*

PASSPORT TO CHILE (page 126) *Grapefruit • lime • hot sauce*

More drinks to make with reposado tequila:

EL GALLITO (page 28) *Pineapple • cherry tomato • chipotle • cilantro*

GORILLA MONSOON (page 47) *Garam masala • mango chutney • tonic*

More drinks to make with mezcal:

OLIVIA FLIP (page 72) *Olive oil • egg • lemon • demerara*

TIBURON (page 73) *Honey • lime • Tabasco • salt*

GRILLED MARGARITA (page 78) *Grilled lemons • honey*

HOY-HOY! (page 109) *Ginger • lemon • orange*

CHILI CHILLY BANG BANG

MAKES 1 DRINK

In the wrong hands, coconutty drinks can be two-dimensional: one dimension is heavy, and the other is sweet. But tiki maven Mindy Kucan of Hale Pele in Portland wouldn't lead us astray, and this frozen delight is beautifully balanced, spicy, and fresh. It calls for vibrant mint and sriracha, fresh pineapple and lime, but it starts with old-school creamy-sweet Coco López, which you'll often find near the mixers in your supermarket. Don't sub in unsweetened coconut milk; it doesn't properly thicken the drink and the flavor just won't pop in the same way.

Before you get started, make sure your Coco López is properly emulsified: plop the unopened can into a bowl with some hot water for a few minutes to soften, then shake, empty it into your blender, and blend until smooth. There's no need to get out a juicer for this; just muddle two 2-inch chunks of fresh pineapple and strain through a fine-mesh strainer, or whir your pineapple in the blender before straining.

2 ounces light rum

1½ ounces fresh lime juice

1 ounce Coco López (blended, see headnote)

1 ounce 1:1 simple syrup (page 13)

¾ ounce fresh pineapple juice

2 teaspoons finely grated fresh ginger

20 fresh mint leaves

1 squirt sriracha, or more to taste

GARNISH: lime wheel and mint sprig

Combine rum, lime juice, Coco López, simple syrup, pineapple juice, ginger, mint, and sriracha in a blender. Add 10 ounces crushed or cubed ice and blend just until you don't hear big chunks bouncing around, about 45 seconds. Pour into a pilsner glass or other large, tall glass. Garnish with a lime wheel and mint sprig.

CAN'T ELOPE IN PANAMA

MAKES 1 DRINK

When melons are in season, it's hard to beat their juicy, subtly floral flavor in drinks. (For the most part, winter's imported melons need not apply.) If you get your hands on a good cantaloupe, make this drink a priority. Muddle up a few melon cubes, amp up the juice with lime and sugar, and shake it all with rum and a few aromatic cilantro leaves for a play on the daiquiri that's really easy to love, especially on a hot summer evening when you've cut out of work early. Bartender Justin Elliott created this recipe for Chauhan Ale and Masala House in Nashville. I like to add a pinch of flaky salt on top.

4 (2-inch) cubes ripe cantaloupe

1½ ounces light rum

½ ounce fresh lime juice

½ ounce 1:1 simple syrup (page 13)

3 fresh cilantro leaves

GARNISH:
fresh cilantro leaf and pinch Maldon salt (optional)

Muddle the cantaloupe in a cocktail shaker until well broken up. Add rum, lime juice, simple syrup, and cilantro and fill with ice. Shake until well chilled, about 15 seconds. Double-strain into a chilled coupe or Nick and Nora glass. Garnish with cilantro leaf and salt if desired.

CASTOR'S GOLD

MAKES 1 DRINK

You might not think of putting horseradish in your coupe glass. But bartender Adam James Sarkis of Phoenix Cocktail Club in downtown Milwaukee shows us how it should be done in this sweet-and-sour cocktail named after the Nicholas Cage character in *Face/Off*. It's a little savory but not too pungent, nicely softened by the honey and lime. Light rum adds velvety richness, but you can also make this drink with vodka.

2 ounces light rum
¾ ounce 2:1 honey syrup (page 14)
¾ ounce fresh lime juice
Scant ¼ teaspoon prepared horseradish (not cream style)

Combine rum, honey syrup, lime juice, and horseradish in a cocktail shaker and fill with ice. Shake vigorously until well chilled, about 15 seconds. Double-strain into a chilled coupe or martini glass.

STONES
AND LEAVES

MAKES 1 DRINK

This one's worth waiting for. When peaches are in season and dripping with sweet juices, slice one up for this cocktail, courtesy of Jesse Carr, bar director of Balise and La Petite Grocery in New Orleans. Carr pairs the luscious stone fruit with honey and rum, then cuts the drink's heady richness with fresh anise-scented Thai basil. Give it a healthy sprig of leaves for garnish: the scent here is essential.

⅓ ripe peach, sliced

½ ounce 2:1 honey syrup (page 14)

2 ounces light rum

½ ounce fresh lemon juice

6 fresh Thai basil leaves

GARNISH: fresh Thai basil sprig, with flowers if available, and freshly ground nutmeg

Muddle peach slices with honey syrup in a cocktail shaker until peaches are broken up. Add rum, lemon juice, and Thai basil and fill with ice. Shake until well chilled, about 15 seconds. Strain into an ice-filled rocks glass. Garnish with Thai basil sprig and freshly ground nutmeg.

MR. TINGLES' PUNCH

MAKES ABOUT 16 DRINKS

There are only a few ingredients in this party-friendly pomegranate-rum punch from John McCarthy of Oran Mor and Greydon House in Nantucket, but each sip is out of the ordinary, with a delicate floral character and a cooling, dancing tingle on your tongue. The key element: a few tablespoons of numbing Sichuan peppercorns, which you spoon into a full bottle of light rum the day before your party. (Inverting the bottle occasionally offers all the fun of a snow globe, but with alcohol and spices instead of snow.)

1 (750 ml) bottle light rum

2 tablespoons Sichuan peppercorns

25 ounces pomegranate juice

8 ½ ounces fresh lemon juice

8 ½ ounces 1:1 simple syrup (page 13)

4 ounces water

GARNISH: ice block, about 20 lemon wheels, ¼ cup pomegranate seeds, and 1 tablespoon each black and pink peppercorns (optional)

At least 24 hours before you plan to serve the punch, fill a Tupperware or cake pan with water and freeze to make an ice block that will fit in your serving vessel, or make several trays of large ice cubes.

Meanwhile, make the infused rum: Carefully spoon Sichuan peppercorns directly into the bottle of rum, using a funnel if desired. Reseal the bottle and let sit at room temperature for 24 hours, jostling occasionally to move the peppercorns around. Strain the infused rum through a fine-mesh strainer and discard peppercorns. If not serving immediately, return the infused rum to the bottle using a funnel and store in a cool, dark place for up to 3 months.

When ready to serve, combine entire bottle of infused rum with the measured pomegranate juice, lemon juice, simple syrup, and water in a large punch bowl. Stir well to mix and carefully add the ice block. Garnish punch bowl with lemon wheels, pomegranate seeds, and peppercorns if using. Ladle into ice-filled punch glasses and garnish each glass with a lemon wheel.

MIDNIGHT IN THE GARDEN

MAKES 1 DRINK

The combination of strawberries and balsamic vinegar shouldn't be dismissed as a '90s salad cliché. The flavors work wonderfully together in the context of a drink like this one from Jeremy Simpson of Ostrich Farm and Bar Calo in Los Angeles. The sweet-tart strawberries mellow out with a few minutes on the stovetop, rounding off any harshness in the vinegar. Shaken with mint and light rum, the combination strikes a refreshing balance of bright flavors and deep ones. If you want to offer a booze-free alternative, the gastrique is also nice mixed with fresh lime juice and chilled club soda.

2 ounces light rum

¾ ounce fresh lime juice

½ ounce strawberry gastrique (see recipe)

5 fresh mint leaves

GARNISH: long lime twist

Combine rum, lime juice, strawberry gastrique, and mint in a cocktail shaker and fill with ice. Shake until well chilled, about 12 seconds. Double-strain into an ice-filled rocks glass and garnish with lime twist.

STRAWBERRY GASTRIQUE

MAKES ABOUT 4½ OUNCES, ENOUGH FOR 9 DRINKS

3 medium or 4 small ripe strawberries (about 2 ounces)
¼ cup water
¼ cup sugar
¼ cup balsamic vinegar

Remove any leaves and chop strawberries. Combine strawberries and water in a small saucepan and cook over medium heat, stirring until berries begin to break down, 6 to 7 minutes. Add sugar and vinegar, turn heat to low, and cook, stirring constantly, until sugar has dissolved, about 1 minute. Remove from heat and let cool for 30 minutes. Strain through a fine-mesh strainer set over a resealable container, pressing on solids to extract juice. Refrigerate for up to 3 days.

SHE'S MY CHERRY PIE

MAKES 6 DRINKS

Like a cherry pie or cobbler tricked out with spicy ginger and robust molasses, this punch bubbles with ripe, fruity flavors that are sharpened with a touch of mouth-puckering lemon and fizzy kombucha. Created by Shaun Gordon of 18.21 Bitters and the James Room in Atlanta, Georgia, it's the perfect offering for a barbecue on a sweltering summer day. Keep in mind that the drink will continue to dilute as it sits on ice.

36 pitted ripe cherries

1 (3-inch) knob fresh ginger, peeled and sliced

18 ounces water

6 ounces fresh lemon juice

4½ ounces 1:1 simple syrup (page 13)

¾ ounce blackstrap molasses

12 ounces light rum

12 ounces chilled ginger-berry kombucha (such as GT's Synergy Gingerberry)

GARNISH: 6 cocktail picks, each speared with cherry and lemon twist

Combine cherries, ginger, water, lemon juice, simple syrup, and molasses in a blender and blend until uniform. Strain through a fine-mesh strainer into a 3-quart pitcher. Stir in rum and refrigerate, covered, for up to 2 hours.

When ready to serve, stir refrigerated mix well. Pour in kombucha and give the mixture another brief, gentle stir. Add ice to pitcher and pour into ice-filled punch or collins glasses, garnishing each glass with a speared cherry and lemon twist.

JOHN PHILLIPS' PUNCH

MAKES ABOUT 8 DRINKS

Shaun Traxler of Sideways in Fayetteville, Arkansas, sometimes adds cream of coconut to this pitcher drink, but I like its easy tropical style without the rich stuff. This one's a crowd-pleaser: carrot juice adds backbone and a bass note to balance the citrus, while a few cans of guava nectar take you all the way to the beach. If you don't want to fuss with a juicer, you can purchase carrot juice at many juice bars and grocery stores. Avoid vegetable blends: you just want carrots here.

16 ounces light rum

16 ounces guava nectar (such as Kern's)

8 ounces fresh orange juice

8 ounces 1:1 simple syrup (page 13)

6 ounces fresh carrot juice

6 ounces fresh lime juice

GARNISH: 10 lime wheels

Stir together rum, guava nectar, orange juice, simple syrup, carrot juice, and lime juice in a 2-quart pitcher or resealable container. Cover and refrigerate for up to 2 hours.

When ready to serve, carefully add ice and lime wheels to pitcher and stir gently. Pour into ice-filled punch glasses.

MY MY MY TAI

MAKES 1 DRINK

The mai tai, a flagship of the tiki oeuvre, is the perfect vacation drink—if you happen to have orgeat and curaçao on hand at your beach rental. This clever version from Jason Saura of Heartwood Provisions and Navy Strength in Seattle subs in grocery store staples like almond milk and marmalade, and it ends up tasting completely credible: funky with rum, bright and citrusy, subtly scented with almond, and nowhere near too sweet. It's a great trick to have up your sleeve. Pssssst: while it's not tiki-traditional, this drink formula is also surprisingly delicious with bourbon.

2 ounces aged rum

1 ounce unsweetened almond milk

1 ounce fresh lime juice

2 tablespoons orange marmalade

GARNISH: mint sprig and lime wedge

Combine rum, almond milk, lime juice, and marmalade in a cocktail shaker and fill with ice. Shake until very well chilled, about 15 seconds. Double-strain into an ice-filled rocks glass. Garnish with mint and lime wedge.

HOY-HOY!

MAKES 1 DRINK

Bartenders add salt to cocktails to round off the bitter edges and help the drink's flavors blossom. Here, Liam Odien of the Corner Door in Culver City goes one step further, deepening that saline character and tying it in to dark barrel-aged rum by using soy sauce instead. The result isn't particularly savory, just full flavored, with a spicy blast of fresh ginger and a balanced sweet-and-sour citrus profile. Take advantage of this opportunity to bring out your thrift-store tiki mugs if you've got 'em. Not a tiki collector? If you don't want to mess with crushed ice, this can also be served tall in a cube-filled collins glass or up in a frosty coupe.

Don't substitute ginger syrup or bottled ginger juice here; if you don't have a juicer, see page 82 for notes on making ginger juice by hand.

2 ounces aged rum

¾ ounce 2:1 honey syrup (page 14)

¾ ounce fresh lemon juice

½ ounce fresh orange juice

1 teaspoon fresh ginger juice

8 drops soy sauce

GARNISH: cocktail umbrella, sprinkle of toasted sesame seeds, and straw (optional)

Combine rum, honey syrup, lemon juice, orange juice, ginger juice, and soy sauce in a cocktail shaker and fill with ice. Shake until well chilled, about 12 seconds. Fill a tiki mug or rocks glass with crushed ice and strain cocktail into it, then top with more crushed ice. Garnish with a cocktail umbrella and sesame seeds, serving with a straw if desired.

SPIKE THE KIDDIE TABLE

MAKES 1 DRINK

At some family gatherings, the kid's table is the place to be. Especially if that's where you're sipping this festive concoction from A. Minetta Gould of Ste. Ellie in Denver. It's made with both fizzy and fresh apple cider and spiked with aged rum for a little toasty caramel action. If you're a hardcore whiskey fan, I recommend you also try this one with Scotch or peppery rye. (Some may prefer to add a drop of simple or honey syrup to the whiskey version.) Feel free to multiply the recipe to serve a crowd, but don't shake more than two drinks at a time.

1½ ounces aged rum

¾ ounce fresh apple cider (from the refrigerator aisle)

½ ounce fresh lemon juice

1 ounce chilled sparkling apple cider (such as Martinelli's)

GARNISH: star anise pod

Combine rum, fresh apple cider, and lemon juice in a cocktail shaker and fill with ice. Shake until well chilled, about 12 seconds. Double-strain into a chilled Champagne flute. Top off with sparkling apple cider and garnish with star anise.

PINEAPPLE-GINGER DAIQUIRI PUNCH

MAKES 12 DRINKS

Spicy, fruity, silky, bold: this large-format ginger daiquiri from Tiffany Hernandez of Cosme and Employees Only in New York is worth a little planning ahead, especially because the reward is a party in a punch bowl. Find a ripe pineapple, cube it up, and soak in rum overnight to lend the spirit a rich, juicy flavor.

½ pineapple

1 (750 ml) bottle aged rum

2 ounces hot water

5 ounces undiluted agave nectar

12 ounces fresh lime juice

5 ½ ounces fresh ginger juice (see page 82)

GARNISH: ice block, about 18 lime wheels, 6 orange wheels, and additional pineapple cubes (optional)

At least 24 hours before you plan to serve the punch, fill a Tupperware or cake pan with water and freeze to make an ice block that will fit in your serving vessel, or make several trays of large ice cubes.

Meanwhile, infuse the rum: Peel pineapple half, discard the core, and cut into 2-inch cubes. Place in a large resealable container. Add rum, making sure pineapple is completely covered. Seal and refrigerate for at least 12 hours and up to 36 hours. Strain the infused rum through a fine-mesh strainer set over another resealable container, pressing on solids to extract juice. Discard pineapple solids. If not serving right away, refrigerate infused rum for up to 3 days.

Up to 2 hours before serving, stir together the hot water and agave nectar to loosen in a large punch bowl and let cool. Add entire batch pineapple-infused rum, lime juice, and ginger juice and stir until well mixed. Serve immediately or cover and refrigerate.

When ready to serve, carefully add ice block or ice cubes to large punch bowl. Garnish with 6 lime wheels, orange wheels, and pineapple chunks if desired. Ladle into ice-filled punch glasses and garnish each with a lime wheel.

NEW WORLD SPRITZ

MAKES 12 DRINKS

Everyone needs a pretty pink pitcher drink for serving at brunches and barbecues; this one from Nathan Shearer of Bar Swift in London will please both cocktail newbies and seasoned sippers. Watermelon adds a fresh fruity flavor, while rum contributes a touch of vanilla (and depending on which rum you pick, a little funky richness). Tonic water helps each sip conclude on a mouthwateringly crisp and just slightly bitter note. To make the watermelon juice, simply process chunks of seedless watermelon in a blender, then strain through a fine-mesh strainer—one medium melon will yield enough juice for the 12-drink batch.

12 ounces aged rum

18 ounces strained watermelon juice (from 1 seedless watermelon)

6 ounces fresh lime juice

6 ounces 1:1 simple syrup (page 13)

30 ounces chilled tonic water

GARNISH: 12 cucumber wheels (from 1 to 2 seedless cucumbers)

Combine rum, watermelon juice, lime juice, and simple syrup in a resealable container and stir well to mix. If not serving right away, cover and refrigerate for up to 2 hours.

Carefully pour tonic water into a 2½-quart pitcher. Stir watermelon mix well, then add to the pitcher as well. Give it a brief, gentle stir and pour into ice-filled collins glasses. Garnish each glass with a cucumber wheel.

TANGO NUEVO

MAKES 1 DRINK

If your salted caramel affogato were a cocktail, well, this is what it would taste like. Roasty coffee and aged rum were made for each other, but the really brilliant part of this drink from Andrew Moore of Ox in Portland is the addition of two pinches of smoked sea salt. One gets stirred in, the other is sprinkled on top of the ice just before serving. This drink practically turns your tongue upside down, hitting all the right notes: savory, salty, sweet, dark. Consider serving it after a meal, alongside good vanilla ice cream garnished with a drizzle of olive oil and a little more of that salt if you're really going over the top. If you truly can't find smoked salt, you can also make this drink with Maldon or other flaky salt.

1 ½ ounces **aged rum**

½ ounce **1:1 honey syrup** (page 14)

½ ounce **unsweetened cold-brew coffee** (such as Stumptown)

Pinch **smoked sea salt**

Splash chilled **club soda**

GARNISH: pinch smoked salt and lemon twist

Combine rum, honey syrup, coffee, and smoked salt in a cocktail shaker and fill with ice. Stir until well chilled, about 30 revolutions. Strain into a rocks glass over a big ice cube and add club soda. Sprinkle a pinch of smoked salt on top of the ice cube and garnish with a lemon twist.

OFFSEASON

MAKES 1 DRINK

Someday, I'd love to be on a long vacation, leaning into a deck chair that sits in a few inches of turquoise infinity-pool water, gazing off into the ocean beyond and sipping this caramelly, tart, and tropical rum drink from Darwin Pornel of Faith and Flower in Los Angeles. Until then, this cocktail works as a nightly escape in a glass, so I've been batching up the fried banana puree in advance. (It's also great stirred into plain yogurt for a little bananas Foster flavor.) If you don't have aged rum on hand, this drink also benefits from bourbon's vanilla notes.

1½ ounces aged rum

1 ounce banana puree
(see recipe)

1 ounce fresh lime juice

½ ounce 1:1 simple syrup
(page 13)

GARNISH: lime wheel

Combine rum, banana puree, lime juice, and simple syrup in a cocktail shaker and shake without ice until emulsified, about 10 seconds. Add ice, reseal shaker, and shake vigorously until well chilled, about 15 seconds. Double-strain into a chilled coupe glass. Garnish with a lime wheel.

BANANA PUREE

MAKES ABOUT 4 OUNCES, ENOUGH FOR 4 DRINKS

1½ ounces hot water

3 tablespoons demerara sugar

¼ cup canola or grapeseed oil

20 slices ripe banana (about 1½ cups)

Combine hot water and sugar in a small mason jar or other resealable container and shake until sugar is dissolved.

Pour the oil into a sauté pan and warm over high heat. Add banana slices in a single layer and, watching carefully, fry until golden brown, 2 to 3 minutes per side. Using a slotted spatula, transfer bananas to a plate.

Combine sautéed bananas and demerara syrup in a food processor or blender and process until uniform. Let cool, then refrigerate in a sealed container for up to 3 days.

BONUS DRINKS

Try substituting rum for the spirit in the drinks below.

More drinks to make with light rum:

WALKABOUT (page 22) *Tangerine • honey • turmeric*

SILKEN SOUR (page 33) *Lime juice • silken tofu*

THE BANGKOK (page 56) *Lemongrass • chile • lemon • mint*

SUN-KISSED HIGHBALL (page 65) *Aloe vera • lime • soda*

GRILLED MARGARITA (page 78) *Grilled lemons • honey*

PART-TIME MODEL (page 129) *Kiwi • cardamom*

More drinks to make with aged rum:

SLIPPERY WHEN WET (page 38) *Strawberry • lemon • Greek yogurt • black pepper*

AROUND THE WAY (page 136) *Peach • thyme • lemon*

NEAR MISS (page 159) *Raspberry • grapefruit peel • lemon*

BOURBON IN BLACK (page 166) *Blackberry • cider vinegar • lavender • honey*

GARDEN COLLINS

MAKES 1 DRINK

We'll start fresh, with pisco, the aromatic, floral-tasting, grape-based brandy that's made in Peru and Chile. In this drink, it brings out the warm sweetness of an unlikely pairing of red bell peppers and ripe cantaloupe. If you've ever wrapped slices of melon with salty prosciutto, you know how a savory partner can make cantaloupe taste even more juicy and intense. The same principle works in this drink from Nathaniel Smith of Spoon and Stable in Minneapolis; the touch of vegetable juice and a pinch of smoked salt make for a fruity cocktail like no other. If you have an electric juicer stashed away, lug it out for this drink; if not, you can blend your melon and bell pepper (separately) in a blender and strain through a fine-mesh strainer. Feel free to double the recipe, but if you want to scale bigger, shake only two drinks at a time.

2 ounces pisco

1 ounce fresh
cantaloupe juice

¾ ounce fresh lime juice

¾ ounce red bell pepper
syrup (see recipe)

Pinch smoked salt or
kosher salt

Splash of chilled
club soda (optional)

GARNISH:
thin bell pepper slice

Combine pisco, cantaloupe juice, lime juice, bell pepper syrup, and smoked salt in a cocktail shaker and fill with ice. Shake until well chilled, about 12 seconds. Add bell pepper slice to a collins glass and fill with ice. Strain cocktail into prepared glass. Add club soda if desired and give it a gentle stir.

RED BELL PEPPER SYRUP

MAKES 3 OUNCES, ENOUGH FOR 4 DRINKS

2 ounces red bell pepper juice (from 1 large or 2 small red bell peppers)
¼ cup sugar

Combine bell pepper juice and sugar in a mason jar or other resealable container with a tight-fitting lid and shake vigorously until sugar is dissolved. Use immediately or refrigerate for up to 2 hours.

PEAR JORDAN

MAKES 2 DRINKS

If I ran a fancy restaurant, I'd want this elegant spin on the pisco sour to be its signature fall cocktail. Created by Los Angeles bartender Nick Meyer, it steers away from most of the standard (often overpowering) autumn spices. Instead, pisco and frothy egg white bring out the mellow floral character of ripe pears. It's easy to make fresh pear juice without a juicer: just whiz up peeled pear segments in a blender and pass the liquid through a fine-mesh strainer.

4 ounces pisco

1½ ounces fresh ripe Bartlett pear juice

1 ounce 1:1 simple syrup (page 13)

¾ ounce fresh lemon juice

¾ ounce fresh lime juice

2 star anise pods

1 egg white

GARNISH: 2 thin pear slices

Combine pisco, pear juice, simple syrup, lemon juice, lime juice, star anise, and egg white in a cocktail shaker and shake without ice until emulsified, about 20 seconds. Add ice, reseal shaker, and shake vigorously until well chilled, about 30 seconds. Strain into 2 chilled large coupe glasses. Balance a pear slice on the rim of each glass.

PASSPORT TO CHILE

MAKES ABOUT 12 DRINKS

You can serve this easy-drinking grapefruit cocktail from Matt Friedlander of New York's Sweetwater Social in a punch bowl with a big ice block. But I like to prep the mix in advance, stash it in the fridge in a pitcher, then pour it into ice-filled glasses. Be sure to have an ice bucket on the side so people can add more ice to their glasses when they pour a second round.

I love how pisco highlights the honey and grapefruit flavors here—but you can also make this easy, citrusy drink with vodka or blanco tequila. If you have an electric citrus juicer, you can save some time. Otherwise, you'll want to put some of your guests to work with a squeezer.

1 (750 ml) bottle pisco

11 ounces 2:1 honey syrup (page 14)

22 ounces fresh grapefruit juice

11 ounces fresh lime juice

½ teaspoon Cholula or other hot sauce

GARNISH: 6 grapefruit wheels, sliced in half, and flaky salt (such as Maldon)

Pour pisco, honey syrup, grapefruit juice, lime juice, and hot sauce into a 2½- or 3-quart pitcher and stir well to mix. If not serving right away, cover and refrigerate for up to 2 hours.

When ready to serve, stir well and pour into ice-filled rocks glasses. Garnish each glass with a half-moon of grapefruit and a pinch of flaky salt.

PART-TIME MODEL

MAKES 1 DRINK

Brandy loves subtle flavors: a whisper of spice, a touch of fruit. Here, floral pisco blends seamlessly into aromatic green cardamom and cooling kiwi. Created by Anna Moss of La Moule in Portland and named with a nod to *Flight of the Conchords*, it's a hot-day, shoes-off sipper, perfect for serving with skewers of grilled shrimp or chicken satay.

2 ounces pisco

1 ounce kiwi-cardamom syrup (see recipe)

¾ ounce fresh lime juice

1 ounce chilled club soda

GARNISH:
kiwi slice (optional)

Combine pisco, kiwi-cardamom syrup, and lime juice in a cocktail shaker and fill with ice. Shake until well chilled, about 12 seconds. Unseal shaker, and add club soda. Strain into an ice-filled rocks glass and garnish with a kiwi slice if desired.

KIWI-CARDAMOM SYRUP
MAKES ABOUT 6 OUNCES, ENOUGH FOR 6 DRINKS

6 whole green cardamom pods
2 kiwis, peeled and sliced
½ cup water
½ cup sugar

In a small saucepan, bash cardamom pods with a muddler to break open. Add kiwis and muddle until a paste forms. (This is easier to do with the saucepan on a counter or cutting board rather than balanced on your stovetop.) Add water and sugar and bring just to a simmer over medium heat, stirring to dissolve sugar and prevent the bottom from burning. As soon as you spot the first bubble, remove pan from heat. Cover and let cool for 20 minutes. Strain syrup through a fine-mesh strainer set over a resealable container, pressing on solids to extract juice. Refrigerate for up to 2 days.

LAST NIGHT IN PERU

MAKES 1 DRINK

This cocktail from Alex Fletcher of Henry's Majestic (and the hidden Atwater Alley) in Dallas is the attractive stranger sitting at the other end of the bar, the one with the soft brown eyes that might be green in another light. She seems familiar somehow, but you can't quite put your finger on why. There's a touch of mystery in each sip here: the muddled dates have a malty caramel flavor that's draped in soft egg white foam and the delicately floral perfume of pisco and orange peel. Don't let this one get away.

4 dried dates

¾ ounce fresh lime juice

2 ounces pisco

¾ ounce 1:1 simple syrup (page 13)

1 egg white

GARNISH: orange twist

Slice dates into quarters, removing any pits. Muddle the quartered dates with the lime juice in a cocktail shaker until well broken up. Add pisco, simple syrup, and egg white and shake without ice until emulsified, about 20 seconds. Add ice, reseal shaker, and shake vigorously until very well chilled, about 30 seconds. Don't quit early! Double-strain into a chilled coupe glass. Squeeze the twist gently over the glass to express orange oils over the top and use as a garnish.

DREAMS OF ASSAM

MAKES 1 DRINK

This soothing take on hot buttered rum gets its understated richness and subtle flavor from coconut butter, which is a mix of coconut oil and pureed coconut meat that's a popular smoothie addition. (You can find it at health food stores and even Whole Foods these days.) Rather than adding spices one by one, Jesse Cyr of Rob Roy in Seattle steeps a spiced black tea bag in hot water, then pours in just enough Cognac (or rye or bourbon, if you prefer) to warm you from the inside out.

Coconut butter often separates at room temperature, so it helps to warm the jar gently in a microwave or bowl of hot water in order to stir it together before you begin.

6 ounces boiling water

1 chai or other black spiced tea bag

1½ ounces Cognac

1 sugar cube or 1 teaspoon sugar

1 teaspoon stirred coconut butter

Pour measured boiling water over tea bag in a preheated mug and steep for 6 minutes. Remove tea bag and add Cognac, sugar cube, and coconut butter, stirring until sugar is dissolved.

A SIDECAR NAMED DESIRE

MAKES 1 DRINK

Find the best apricot jam you can. Maybe it's at the farmers' market, maybe you mail-order it from California's Frog Hollow Farm, maybe your neighbor makes his own every summer. When you get your hands on the good stuff (or a decent sugar-sweetened version like Bonne Maman), make this drink, pronto. Created by Laura Bellucci, who runs the bar program at SoBou in the heart of the French Quarter of New Orleans, this cocktail riffs on the classic sidecar, with a huge boost of summery flavor from that rich stone fruit. If you have Angostura bitters around, feel free to add a few dashes before shaking for a touch of extra spice. It doesn't need it, though.

2 ounces Cognac

3 tablespoons top-quality apricot jam

½ ounce fresh lemon juice

GARNISH: lemon twist

Combine Cognac, jam, and lemon juice in a cocktail shaker and fill with ice. Shake vigorously until well chilled, about 12 seconds. Double-strain into a chilled coupe glass. Gently squeeze the lemon twist over the top of the drink to express oils, then use as a garnish.

FRENCH CANADIAN

MAKES 1 DRINK

Many bartenders hesitated when I told them I wanted to write a book collecting single-bottle recipes. How can you make anything like a cocktail—especially a stirred one—without vermouth, without liqueur? This drink is the perfect proof of concept, created by Nathan Shearer of Bar Swift in London. Cognac gets stirred with tangy champagne vinegar, sweet maple syrup, and aromatic vanilla extract for a cocktail that's silky and potent, perfect for serving after a meal. If you prefer your cocktails on the drier side, use the larger quantity of Cognac.

2 to 2 ¼ ounces Cognac

¼ ounce **champagne vinegar**

¼ ounce **maple syrup**

¼ teaspoon **pure vanilla extract**

GARNISH: lemon twist

Combine Cognac, vinegar, maple syrup, and vanilla in a mixing glass and fill with ice. Stir until well chilled, about 30 revolutions. Strain into a chilled coupe glass, gently squeeze the lemon twist over the top to express oils, then use as a garnish.

AROUND THE WAY

MAKES 1 DRINK

There's a problem with peaches: they're fleeting. For a month or two, these fuzzy fruits grace us with bubbling pies and crumbles and dripping half-moons best eaten over the sink, and then they disappear. But even if you can't get your hands on a fresh peach, this cocktail from Greg Innocent of the Bassment in Chicago is a pretty good consolation prize. Peach nectar, which you can buy bottled or boxed year-round, subtly boosts the stone fruit flavors in Cognac. Fresh thyme steeped in warm simple syrup gives the combination a sophisticated herbal edge. I also like this drink with peppery rye as the base, or aged rum, which makes the whole thing taste even more peachy.

2 ounces Cognac

¾ ounce thyme syrup (see recipe)

¾ ounce fresh lemon juice

½ ounce peach juice or peach nectar (such as Ceres)

GARNISH: thyme sprig

Combine Cognac, thyme syrup, lemon juice, and peach juice in a cocktail shaker and fill with ice. Shake until well chilled, about 12 seconds. Strain into an ice-filled rocks glass. Garnish with a thyme sprig.

THYME SYRUP
MAKES ABOUT 9 OUNCES, ENOUGH FOR 12 DRINKS

¾ cup water
¾ cup sugar
12 thyme sprigs

Combine water, sugar, and thyme in a small saucepan and cook over medium heat, stirring until sugar dissolves. Let come to a bare simmer, then remove from heat and let sit for 30 minutes. Strain through a fine-mesh strainer into a resealable container and discard thyme. Refrigerate for up to 1 week.

DAISY 77

MAKES 12 DRINKS

Iced chamomile tea with honey in it always tastes sunny, evoking pollen in the breeze as you tromp through the dirt on a warm afternoon. These earthy qualities are right at home with the toffee-and-nuts character of Cognac, and that's basically all you need to craft this easy punch from Patrick Poelvoorde of Burritt Room and Tavern in San Francisco. If you don't have a punch bowl, you can also serve this in a 2-quart pitcher.

2 chamomile tea bags

3 ounces boiling water

3 ounces honey

18 ounces Cognac

9 ounces fresh lemon juice

18 ounces chilled club soda

GARNISH: large cubes of ice or ice block, about 20 lemon wheels, 5 edible flowers (optional), and 12 thyme sprigs

At least 24 hours before you plan to serve the punch, fill a Tupperware or cake pan with water and freeze to make an ice block that will fit in your serving vessel, or make several trays of large ice cubes.

Steep tea bags in boiling water for 4 minutes. Remove tea bags and add honey, stirring until fully incorporated. Let cool and use immediately or refrigerate for up to 1 week.

Up to 3 hours before serving, combine Cognac, lemon juice, and entire batch chamomile-honey mixture in a punch bowl and stir well to mix. Serve immediately or cover and refrigerate for up to 3 hours.

When ready to serve, pour in club soda and give the punch a brief, gentle stir. Carefully add ice block or cubes and garnish bowl with lemon wheels and edible flowers if using. Ladle punch into ice-filled punch glasses or wine glasses and garnish each glass with a thyme sprig.

FRENCH JULEP

MAKES 1 DRINK

Cognac always reminds me a bit of malt and honey, and figs have a complementary, slightly nutty profile. David Perez of Nancy in Miami puts them together in this smooth operator, which is shaken with mint leaves so each sip finishes bright and clean. If you don't have julep cups, no sweat; rocks glasses work fine, too, as long as they are piled high with crushed ice. While bourbon is a little too sweet here, this drink is quite tasty with rye or Scotch instead of the brandy.

2 ounces Cognac

¾ ounce fresh lemon juice

½ ounce 2:1 honey syrup (page 14)

1 teaspoon fig preserves

8 fresh mint leaves

GARNISH:
mint sprig and a straw

Combine Cognac, lemon juice, honey syrup, fig preserves, and mint in a cocktail shaker and fill with ice. Shake vigorously until well chilled, about 20 seconds. Fill a julep cup with crushed ice and double-strain cocktail into it. Garnish with mint sprig and a straw.

WELCOME, DOROTHY

MAKES 2 DRINKS

I first met Caitlin Laman, who created this drink, when she was the bar manager at Trick Dog, the cocktail destination that just happens to be a few steps from my house in San Francisco. These days, you'll find her in Chicago at the Ace Hotel.

This fruity, subtly savory concoction requires no muddling: when you shake quartered ripe strawberries along with booze and lemon juice, the berries begin to dissolve (a double-strain gets rid of the seeds before you start sipping). The fruit gets an intriguing leathery vanilla-and-tobacco note from rooibos, which you'll find in the tea aisle of most gourmet grocery or health food stores.

3 ounces
Cognac or Armagnac

1½ ounces
fresh lemon juice

1½ ounces 1:1 simple syrup
(page 13)

4 ripe
strawberries, quartered

4 ounces brewed
rooibos tea, cooled

GARNISH:
2 thin lemon wheels

Combine Cognac, lemon juice, simple syrup, and strawberries in a cocktail shaker and fill with ice. Shake vigorously until well chilled, about 25 seconds. Add tea to shaker and give it a brief, gentle stir. Double-strain into 2 ice-filled 10-ounce collins glasses. Garnish each glass with a lemon wheel.

BONUS DRINKS

Try substituting brandy for the spirit in the drinks below.

More drinks to make with pisco:

JE NE SAIS QUOI (page 42) *Green grapes • tarragon*

BAY OF BENGAL (page 52) *Coconut • rice milk • curry powder*

THE BANGKOK (page 56) *Lemongrass • chile • lemon • mint*

SHE'S MY CHERRY PIE (page 104) *Cherries • ginger •
blackstrap molasses • kombucha*

More drinks to make with cognac:

THE GINCIDENT (page 45) *Blueberries • basil • rosemary • lemon*

TANGO NUEVO (page 117) *Coffee • smoked salt • honey*

OFFSEASON (page 118) *Fried banana • lime*

CRANBERRY IN A CAN (page 153) *Cranberry • cinnamon •
champagne vinegar*

NEAR MISS (page 159) *Raspberry • grapefruit peel • lemon*

BREAKFAST OF CHAMPIONS (page 162) *Honey Nut
Cheerios • milk • cinnamon*

SPANISH PENNY

MAKES 1 DRINK

This effortless stirred drink from Andrew M. Volk of the Portland Hunt and Alpine Club in Maine celebrates the rye barrel and the sherry cask. Potent, peppery whiskey (Volk recommends seeking out a 100-proof rye) mingles with a crisp touch of sherry vinegar, but the key to the perfect mix is a softening spoonful of maple syrup. The drink comes together silky and rich, with a lingering maple flavor that's perfect for a cool evening.

2 ounces rye
(100 proof preferred)

1 teaspoon maple syrup

¼ teaspoon sherry vinegar

GARNISH: dried apricot
on a cocktail pick (optional)

Combine rye, maple syrup, and sherry vinegar in a rocks glass and fill with ice. Stir until chilled, about 30 revolutions. Garnish with a speared apricot.

GOLDEN LION TAMARIN

MAKES 1 DRINK

I have a soft spot for the vanilla-scented, butterscotch flavors of cream soda, but these days it usually tastes too sweet to me for more than a sip or two. This drink from Jason Saura of Heartwood Provisions and Navy Strength in Seattle hits the ideal balance. Spicy rye (a high-proof one like Rittenhouse is great here) and hot ginger blast through the soda's sugar, leaving you with a brighter, hotter, more exciting version of the nostalgic drink. This drink works nicely with blended Scotch too.

4 quarter-size slices peeled fresh ginger

½ ounce fresh lemon juice

2 ounces rye

4 ounces cream soda

GARNISH: 2 lemon wheels

Muddle ginger with lemon juice in a cocktail shaker. Add rye, fill with ice, and shake until well chilled, about 15 seconds. Double-strain into an ice-filled pilsner glass or other large, tall glass. Pour cream soda down the side of the glass and give it a brief, gentle stir. Garnish with lemon wheels.

THE
BLUEST CHAI

MAKES 1 DRINK

Making the gingery, cinnamony, cardamom- and clove-laced syrup for this whiskey drink from Trevor Frye of Five to One in Washington, D.C., is as easy as making tea—all you do is throw a chai tea bag in some hot water, then stir in some sugar. The chai gives the cocktail a warm-spice flavor that's rounded out with tangy balsamic vinegar. There's no need to shell out for high-end aged balsamic here; in fact, those concentrated versions can make the drink a touch too sweet. For the non-tipplers in your crowd, skip the whiskey and shake an ounce of the chai syrup with 1 ¼ ounces lemon juice and ½ teaspoon balsamic, then top with club soda.

1 ½ ounces rye

¾ ounce chai syrup (see recipe)

¾ ounce fresh lemon juice

1 teaspoon balsamic vinegar

Pinch salt

GARNISH: lemon twist

Combine rye, chai syrup, lemon juice, balsamic vinegar, and salt in a cocktail shaker and fill with ice. Shake until well chilled, about 12 seconds. Strain into a chilled coupe glass. Express oils from lemon twist over the top and discard.

CHAI SYRUP
MAKES ABOUT 6 OUNCES, ENOUGH FOR 8 DRINKS

½ cup boiling water

1 chai tea bag

½ cup sugar

Add boiling water and tea bag to a heatproof resealable container with a tight-fitting lid and let steep for 5 minutes. Remove tea bag and add sugar, stirring or shaking until dissolved. Let cool and refrigerate for up to 1 week.

CALIFORNIA CHROME

MAKES 2 DRINKS

This spicy stallion was named for a Kentucky Derby–winning Californian racehorse by Chris Amirault of Otium in Los Angeles. It's a tart, aromatic variation on the grapefruit-laced Brown Derby cocktail, with added backbone from a little lemon juice and a fragrant, lingering warmth from five-spice powder and peppery rye whiskey. The spice packs a punch; if you like your drinks a little more mellow, try scaling down the five-spice powder by a pinch.

4 ounces rye

1 ounce 3:1 honey syrup (page 14)

½ teaspoon five-spice powder

2 ounces fresh grapefruit juice

1 ounce fresh lemon juice

GARNISH: 2 grapefruit twists

Combine rye, honey syrup, five-spice powder, grapefruit juice, and lemon juice in a cocktail shaker and fill with ice. Shake until well chilled, about 15 seconds. Double-strain into 2 chilled coupe glasses and garnish each glass with a grapefruit twist.

CRANBERRY IN A CAN

MAKES 12 DRINKS

Dee Ann Quinones dreamed up this festive drink recipe for the holiday menu at Grace Gaelic Hospitality in New York. It was inspired, she says, by visions of fruitcakes and the cranberry sauce served alongside a rich Thanksgiving feast. It's perfect for wintertime entertaining because you can make the easy cinnamon-spiced cranberry mixer far ahead of the last-minute chaos, add booze, and offer the drink in a pitcher for guests to serve themselves. Don't be afraid of the vinegar: it offers just enough tartness to balance the warm cinnamon and whiskey flavors. If you're not a fan of rye, try Cognac; it makes a satiny-smooth, easy-drinking version of the punch.

24 ounces rye

12 ounces quick cranberry-cinnamon shrub (see recipe)

GARNISH: 12 fresh mint sprigs, 36 fresh cranberries or red currants, and straws

Combine rye and shrub together in a 1½- or 2-quart pitcher and stir well to mix. Pour about 3 ounces into each julep cup or rocks glass. Fill with crushed ice. Garnish each glass with a mint sprig, 3 cranberries or red currants, and a straw.

QUICK CRANBERRY-CINNAMON SHRUB
MAKES ABOUT 12 OUNCES, ENOUGH FOR 12 DRINKS

1 cup sugar
4 ounces unsweetened 100% cranberry juice
4 ounces champagne vinegar
5 cinnamon sticks

Combine sugar, cranberry juice, and vinegar in a small saucepan over medium-high heat and stir well to mix. Break up cinnamon sticks and add to the syrup. Stir constantly for about 5 minutes to dissolve sugar and bring mixture to a bare simmer, then remove from heat and let sit, covered, for 30 minutes. Strain through a fine-mesh strainer set over a resealable container and discard cinnamon sticks. Refrigerate shrub for at least 1 hour and up to 1 week.

THE BARKEEP'S BREAKFAST

MAKES 2 DRINKS

John Holzinger, who has gone from Bourbon and Branch in San Francisco to a gig at Michter's Whiskey, gathered morning flavors into this spirit-forward drink: he lets a bag of Earl Grey sit in a jar of rye for a few hours to infuse the whiskey with aromatic bergamot and earthy tea flavors. Stirred with fresh orange juice and honey, it makes an old-fashioned riff that's citrusy, tannic, and delicately spicy.

¼ ounce honey
¼ ounce fresh orange juice
4 ounces
Earl Grey–infused rye
(see recipe)

GARNISH:
freshly grated cinnamon

Combine honey and orange juice in a mixing glass and stir to loosen. Add infused rye and fill with ice. Stir until well chilled, about 30 revolutions. Strain into 2 ice-filled rocks glasses. Garnish each glass with a very light dusting of cinnamon.

EARL GREY–INFUSED RYE
MAKES 8 OUNCES, ENOUGH FOR 4 DRINKS

8 ounces rye
1 Earl Grey tea bag

Combine rye and tea bag in a mason jar or other resealable container. Let sit at room temperature for 2 to 3 hours. Remove tea bag and strain through a fine-mesh strainer set over a resealable container to capture any bits of tea that may have escaped the bag. Infused whiskey will keep for several months.

SWITCHBACK HIGHBALL

MAKES 1 DRINK

It's hard to imagine a better fall cocktail than this simple one from Thomas Spaeth of Dear Irving in New York. Inspired by the switchel, a refreshing vinegar-based drink that goes way, way back, this tart little number brings together apple cider vinegar, lemon juice, maple syrup, and spicy rye (or blended Scotch, if you're in the mood). The sweetness of your drink will depend on your ginger beer; feel free to dial up the maple a little if you're using a particularly dry version.

2 ounces rye

½ ounce apple cider vinegar

½ ounce fresh lemon juice

¼ ounce maple syrup

1½ ounces chilled ginger beer

GARNISH: mint sprig

Combine rye, vinegar, lemon juice, and maple syrup in a cocktail shaker and fill with ice. Shake until chilled, about 10 seconds. Unseal shaker and add ginger beer, then strain into an ice-filled collins glass. Garnish with a mint sprig.

BUTTERMILK FLIP

MAKES 1 DRINK

If eggnog is your go-to holiday beverage, I urge you to try this creamy bourbon cocktail from Brandon Presbury, who created it for Lazy Bear in San Francisco. While it's frothy and egg yolk–enriched like the holiday classic, this drink keeps its maple-sweetened richness in balance, thanks to buttermilk's tang and the bitter cut of cold-brew coffee.

1 ounce bourbon

½ ounce 1:1 diluted maple syrup (page 14)

½ ounce unsweetened cold-brew coffee

½ ounce buttermilk

1 egg

GARNISH: hazelnut, grated on a Microplane or cheese grater

Combine bourbon, diluted maple syrup, coffee, buttermilk, and egg in a cocktail shaker. Shake without ice until emulsified, about 20 seconds, then fill shaker with ice and reseal. Shake vigorously until well chilled and very frothy, about 30 seconds. Double-strain into an ice-filled rocks glass and garnish with grated hazelnut.

NEAR MISS

Benjamin Schiller of The Fifty/50 Restaurant Group in Chicago counters the simple sweetness of fresh raspberries and mint with the power of the peel: both lemon and grapefruit peels, to be exact. Muddling half a lemon and two swaths of grapefruit brings out their aromatic oils and a little bitterness, which keeps this juicy, fruity whiskey cooler in balance. The result is a gorgeous magenta drink that wakes up your taste buds and keeps your mouth watering.

½ lemon, cut into 3 wedges

7 ripe raspberries

¾ ounce 1:1 simple syrup (page 13)

2 grapefruit twists

2 ounces bourbon

Leaves from 1 sprig mint

2 ounces chilled club soda

GARNISH: mint sprig

Combine lemon wedges, raspberries, simple syrup, and grapefruit twists in a cocktail shaker and muddle until raspberries are well broken up. Add bourbon and mint and fill with ice. Shake until very well chilled, about 15 seconds. Double-strain into an ice-filled collins glass, pour the club soda down the side of the glass, and give it a brief, gentle stir. Garnish with a mint sprig.

NEWTON'S LAW

MAKES 1 DRINK

Apple butter is a brilliant shortcut to a robustly flavored drink. Deeply appley, spiced with cinnamon and sometimes ginger, nutmeg, or clove, it brings in every essential autumn note in a teaspoon or two. In this drink from Zach Lynch, bar manager of the Ice Plant in St. Augustine, Florida, the apple butter meets its match in bourbon (plus lemon juice and dark brown sugar to bring out both high and low notes). All that's missing is a pumpkin patch and a freshly fried cider doughnut.

1 teaspoon dark brown sugar

1 teaspoon hot water

1½ ounces bourbon

½ ounce fresh lemon juice

2 teaspoons apple butter

GARNISH:
orange twist and freshly grated or ground cinnamon

Stir together brown sugar and hot water in a cocktail shaker to dissolve. Let cool, then add bourbon, lemon juice, and apple butter and fill with ice. Shake until well chilled, about 15 seconds. Strain into an ice-filled rocks glass. Garnish with orange twist and cinnamon.

BREAKFAST OF CHAMPIONS

MAKES 1 DRINK

Whether or not Honey Nut Cheerios were your favorite accompaniment to Saturday morning cartoons as a kid, this creamy whiskey drink created by Jared Hirsch of NickelDime Syrups and Sidebar in Oakland is too fun to resist. Bourbon slices through the sweet, nutty flavor of the milk left over at the bottom of your cereal bowl, and it's all enlivened with a sprinkle of cinnamon. (Okay, you probably want to actually mix the cereal and milk exclusively for this purpose, especially if you plan to serve this to friends. The infusion is quick and painless, I promise.) Try it with Cognac instead of the whiskey if you have a bottle around.

1½ ounces bourbon

¾ ounce 2:1 honey syrup (page 14)

3 ounces Honey Nut Cheerios–infused milk (see recipe)

GARNISH: freshly grated or ground cinnamon and cocktail pick with skewered Cheerios

Combine bourbon, honey syrup, and Honey Nut Cheerios–infused milk in a cocktail shaker and fill with ice. Shake vigorously until well chilled, about 20 seconds. Double-strain into an ice-filled collins or juice glass and garnish with cinnamon and a cocktail pick with skewered Cheerios.

HONEY NUT CHEERIOS–INFUSED MILK
MAKES ABOUT 7 OUNCES, ENOUGH FOR 2 DRINKS

1 cup Honey Nut Cheerios
8 ounces whole milk

Combine Cheerios and milk in a resealable container. Refrigerate for 1 hour, stirring or shaking occasionally to help Cheerios break down. Strain through a fine-mesh strainer set over a resealable container, pressing on solids to get as much liquid as possible, and refrigerate for up to 2 days.

WOODEN NICKEL

MAKES 1 DRINK

This exquisitely simple drink from Liam Odien of the Corner Door in Culver City brings out the best in all its ingredients. Honey and bourbon are cousins, their richness calling out for tart lemon and tangy tangerine juice. Nothing else is needed. If you can't find tangerines, you can also use sweet little mandarin oranges, but you might want to squeeze in a touch more lemon. Fans of rye whiskey can also try that spirit here.

2 ounces bourbon

¾ ounce 2:1 honey syrup (page 14)

½ ounce fresh lemon juice

½ ounce fresh tangerine juice

GARNISH: wide tangerine twist

Combine bourbon, honey syrup, lemon juice, and tangerine juice in a cocktail shaker. Shake until well chilled, about 12 seconds. Double-strain into a chilled coupe glass and garnish with a tangerine twist.

BITTER GENTLEMAN

MAKES 1 DRINK

This spiritous stirred drink from Michael Neff of The Three Clubs in Los Angeles is for lovers of the classic old-fashioned. Bourbon's vanilla flavors, gained over years resting in toasty barrels, are echoed with a split vanilla bean, and the whiskey's gentle sweetness is cut with a tannic and bitter syrup made with long-steeped Darjeeling tea and a few lemon twists. If you can find dark, malty-tasting buckwheat honey, this is a great place to use it. For non-tipplers, shake an ounce of the bitter tea syrup with ice and an equal amount of lemon juice, then top off with chilled club soda.

2 ounces bourbon
¾ ounce bitter tea syrup (see recipe)

GARNISH: lemon twist

Combine bourbon and bitter tea syrup in a rocks glass. Add 1 large ice cube or fill glass with smaller ice cubes. Stir until well chilled, about 30 revolutions. Garnish with lemon twist.

BITTER TEA SYRUP

MAKES 5 OUNCES, ENOUGH FOR 6 DRINKS

12 ounces water
2 Darjeeling tea bags
2 tablespoons honey
½ vanilla bean, split lengthwise
8 lemon twists

Bring water to a boil in a small saucepan. Remove from heat, add tea bags, and let steep for 10 minutes. Remove tea bags and add honey, stirring until fully incorporated. Return to medium-high heat and simmer, stirring occasionally, until volume is reduced by half, 10 to 12 minutes. Add vanilla bean and lemon twists and simmer for 3 minutes more. Remove from heat, let cool for 10 minutes, then strain through a fine-mesh strainer set over a resealable container. Refrigerate for up to 1 week.

BOURBON IN BLACK

MAKES 8 DRINKS

Hosting a party is stressful enough without fussing over last-minute cocktail prep. This drink from Lynnette Marrero of New York City's Llama Inn (and cofounder of the awesome Speed Rack bartending competition) is perfect for making ahead. A touch of dried lavender boosts the quietly floral flavors of ripe blackberries here. If your grocery store doesn't have dried lavender in the spice aisle, you can substitute lavender tea. The berries are preserved in a simple make-ahead shrub—that is, a sweetened fruit vinegar that's tangy and complex, almost wine-like in flavor, and delicious to sip with sparkling water (or a cup of booze). Marrero recommends bourbon, but I'd be remiss if I didn't mention that you really should also try it with a rich aged rum. (Pro tip: Split the recipe in two so you can offer both versions and have your guests pick a favorite.)

1 tablespoon dried lavender or 1 lavender tea bag

6 tablespoons boiling water

6 tablespoons honey

16 ounces bourbon

8 ounces blackberry shrub (see recipe)

24 ounces chilled club soda

GARNISH: tall fresh lavender sprigs (optional) and 1 cup blackberries

Steep dried lavender or lavender tea bag in measured boiling water for 3 minutes. Strain through a fine-mesh strainer into a resealable container. Add honey, stirring until fully incorporated. Let cool and refrigerate for up to 2 days.

Up to 8 hours before serving, pour lavender honey into a 2- or 2½-quart pitcher. Stir in bourbon and blackberry shrub. If not serving right away, cover tightly and refrigerate for up to 8 hours.

When ready to serve, stir mixture well. Pour in club soda and give the pitcher a brief, gentle stir. Garnish with lavender sprigs if using. Serve cocktail in ice-filled collins or punch glasses, garnishing each with a few blackberries.

BLACKBERRY SHRUB

MAKES ABOUT 16 OUNCES, ENOUGH FOR 16 DRINKS

1 cup ripe blackberries
12 ounces apple cider vinegar
1½ to 2 tablespoons honey, depending on sweetness
of berries

At least 2 days before you plan to use the shrub, clean a
24-ounce mason jar or resealable nonreactive container
with boiling water. Empty container and add blackberries,
smashing slightly with a muddler. Add apple cider vinegar.
Cover and refrigerate for 2 days.

Strain the berry mixture through a fine-mesh strainer set
over a saucepan, pressing on solids to extract juice. Discard
solids. Add 1½ tablespoons honey to the pan and stir over
medium-low heat until the honey dissolves. Taste and
add up to ½ tablespoon more honey if desired; the shrub
should be tart and refreshing. Remove from heat and
let cool. Refrigerate in a resealable container for up to
2 weeks. (Throw it out if any mold appears.)

AULD BOULEVARD

MAKES 1 DRINK

The Boulevardier, a cool-weather relative of the Negroni, is usually made with rye or bourbon, but I love the savory, smoky taste that Scotch contributes. In this take, the Scotch is paired with bittersweet radicchio syrup, a brilliant creation of Zac Overman of L'Oursin in Seattle that's reminiscent of Cynar, the vegetal Italian amaro. For a bracing nonalcoholic option, try mixing ¾ ounce radicchio syrup with 1 ounce fresh white grapefruit juice and 3 ounces tonic.

1 ¾ ounces Scotch

¾ ounce bittersweet radicchio syrup (see recipe)

½ ounce fresh orange juice, strained through a fine-mesh strainer

GARNISH: orange twist

Combine Scotch, radicchio syrup, and orange juice in a rocks glass. Add 1 large ice cube or fill glass with smaller ice cubes. Stir until well chilled, about 30 revolutions. Express oils from orange twist over the top and drop in.

BITTERSWEET RADICCHIO SYRUP
MAKES 10 OUNCES, ENOUGH FOR 13 DRINKS

½ cup sugar
8 ounces water
1 ¾ cups chopped radicchio (about 1 head radicchio)
4 grapefruit twists
10 fresh rosemary leaves

Add sugar and water to a saucepan and bring to a simmer over medium-high heat, stirring until dissolved. Add radicchio (it will seem like a lot, but don't worry!) and stir until leaves are wilted. Reduce heat to keep at a bare simmer and let infuse, stirring occasionally, for 20 minutes. Add grapefruit twists and rosemary and simmer for 5 minutes more. Remove from heat and let cool for 10 minutes. Strain through a fine-mesh strainer set over a resealable container, pressing on solids, then discard solids. Refrigerate for up to 1 week.

KOJI KING

MAKES 1 DRINK

One thing we love about Scotch whisky—sometimes without even realizing it—is the spirit's umami quality. Chicago bartender Julia Momose amplifies that savory factor by shaking Scotch (a lightly peated version works well) with earthy white miso and a rich syrup of caramelly demerara sugar. The resulting cocktail is full and round in the mouth, meaty but also sweet-tart.

1½ ounces Scotch

1 ounce fresh lemon juice

¾ ounce 2:1 demerara simple syrup (page 13)

½ teaspoon white miso paste (such as Miso Master)

GARNISH: lemon twist

Combine Scotch, lemon juice, simple syrup, and miso in a cocktail shaker and fill with ice. Shake until well chilled, about 15 seconds. Double-strain into a chilled coupe or Nick and Nora glass. Express oils from lemon twist over the cocktail and discard.

ON THE SLY

MAKES 1 DRINK

This recipe from North Carolina–based bartender Jenna Jones may read like the formula for a Frappuccino, but it has layered flavors that aren't hidden behind a sugar sludge. Coffee—either brewed strong at home or purchased as cold brew—creates a bitter backbone that's shored up with a pinch of unsweetened cocoa. Allspice contributes a floral note, cayenne a gentle warming heat, and maple a subtle sweetness. This drink works well with blended Scotch, but if you have a peaty Islay like Ardbeg or Laphaoig on hand, sub it in for a quarter ounce or so of the spirit to add a touch of smoke.

2 ounces Scotch
(see headnote)

2 ounces unsweetened
cold-brew or double-
strength brewed coffee,
decaf if desired

¾ ounce maple syrup

½ ounce heavy cream

2 pinches ground allspice

1 pinch unsweetened cocoa

1 pinch cayenne pepper

GARNISH:
1 pinch allspice and
1 pinch cayenne (optional)

Combine Scotch, coffee, maple syrup, heavy cream, allspice, cocoa, and cayenne in a cocktail shaker. Fill with ice and shake vigorously until well chilled and very frothy, about 20 seconds. Strain into a wine glass and garnish with allspice and cayenne if desired.

FULL REGALIA

MAKES 1 DRINK

Peaty Scotch and savory oolong tea work their smoky magic together in this sour created by Jordan Felix of Portland's Multnomah Whiskey Library. It's just barely sweetened with a couple of teaspoons of orange marmalade and topped with a crown of velvety egg white foam. Bittersweet orange and dry tannin linger on your tongue with a whisper of whisky, calling for another sip, and another.

2 ounces Scotch

1 ounce brewed oolong tea, cooled

½ ounce fresh lemon juice

2 teaspoons orange marmalade (such as Bonne Maman)

½ ounce egg white or aquafaba (see page 17)

GARNISH: large orange twist

Combine Scotch, cooled tea, lemon juice, marmalade, and egg white in a cocktail shaker. Shake without ice until well emulsified, at least 30 seconds. Fill shaker with ice and reseal. Shake vigorously until well chilled and very frothy, about 30 more seconds. Double-strain into a chilled coupe glass. Express oils from orange twist over the cocktail and discard.

BO NUS DRINKS

Try substituting whiskey for the spirit in the drinks below.

More drinks to make with rye:

SPIKE THE KIDDIE TABLE (page 110) *Sparkling apple cider • lemon*

DREAMS OF ASSAM (page 131) *Hot chai • coconut butter*

A SIDECAR NAMED DESIRE (page 132) *Apricot jam • lemon*

AROUND THE WAY (page 136) *Peach • thyme • lemon*

DAISY 77 (page 139) *Chamomile • honey • lemon*

FRENCH JULEP (page 140) *Fig preserves • honey • mint • lemon*

More drinks to make with bourbon:

GRILLED MARGARITA (page 78) *Grilled lemons • honey*

MY MY MY TAI (page 107) *Orange marmalade • almond milk • lime*

OFFSEASON (page 118) *Fried banana • lime*

DREAMS OF ASSAM (page 131) *Hot chai • coconut butter*

More drinks to make with Scotch:

SPIKE THE KIDDIE TABLE (page 110) *Sparkling apple cider • lemon*

FRENCH JULEP (page 140) *Fig preserves • honey • mint • lemon*

GOLDEN LION TAMARIN (page 148) *Cream soda • ginger*

SWITCHBACK HIGHBALL (page 156) *Cider vinegar • maple syrup • ginger beer*

DRINKS BY SEASON AND OCCASION

SPRING

Bees in the Trap (21)

Slippery When Wet (38)

Gin Rocket (48)

Boogie Nights (62)

Desert Sunset (89)

Dr. Green Thumb (90)

Midnight in the Garden (103)

French Julep (140)

Welcome, Dorothy (142)

SUMMER

Garden Gnome (24)

Phuket (27)

The Gincident (45)

Sun-Kissed Highball (65)

Can't Elope in Panama (96)

Stones and Leaves (99)

She's My Cherry Pie (104)

New World Spritz (114)

Garden Collins (122)

Near Miss (159)

Bourbon in Black (166)

FALL

Purple Fog (23)

3 Beet High and Rising (41)

Gorilla Monsoon (47)

Bay of Bengal (52)

French Concession (77)

Marrakesh Express (86)

Pear Jordan (125)

The Bluest Chai (150)

Switchback Highball (156)

Newton's Law (160)

WINTER

Walkabout (22)

Olivia Flip (72)

Sassy Flower (81)

Spike the Kiddie Table (110)

Dreams of Assam (131)

Spanish Penny (147)

California Chrome (151)

The Barkeep's Breakfast (154)

Buttermilk Flip (157)

Wooden Nickel (164)

Auld Boulevard (169)

BRIDAL SHOWER BRUNCH

Phuket (27)

Gin Rocket (48)

Rose of All Roses (55)

Boogie Nights (62)

New World Spritz (114)

Passport to Chile (126)

Bourbon in Black (166)

SUPER BOWL PARTY

Police and Thieves (51)

Green Gold (69)

Grilled Margarita (78)

Sassy Flower (81)

Mr. Tingles' Punch (100)

Switchback Highball (156)

Wooden Nickel (164)

VALENTINE'S DAY

Sassy Flower (81)

Heart of Fire (85)

Marrakesh Express (86)

Spike the Kiddie Table (110)

Tango Nuevo (117)

Last Night in Peru (130)

CINCO DE MAYO

El Gallito (28)

Green Gold (69)

Tamarindo Aguas Frescas (70)

Tiburon (73)

La Verduderia (75)

Grilled Margarita (78)

Desert Sunset (89)

FANCY DINNER PARTY

Behind the Field (30)

Gin Rocket (48)

Domo Arigato (82)

Pear Jordan (125)

A Sidecar Named Desire (132)

Daisy 77 (139)

Spanish Penny (147)

Full Regalia (172)

BACKYARD BARBECUE

El Gallito (28)

Sun-Kissed Highball (65)

Tamarindo Aguas Frescas (70)

She's My Cherry Pie (104)

John Phillips' Punch (106)

Pineapple-Ginger Daiquiri Punch (113)

New World Spritz (114)

THANKSGIVING FEAST OR HOLIDAY FÊTE

Purple Fog (23)

Sassy Flower (81)

Spike the Kiddie Table (110)

Mr. Tingles' Punch (100)

Tango Nuevo (117)

Cranberry in a Can (153)

Buttermilk Flip (157)

Full Regalia (172)

WHICH BOTTLE?

The drinks you make are only as good as your ingredients. The bartenders featured in this book recommend the following spirits for mixing.

VODKA

The 86 Co. Aylesbury Duck Vodka

Absolut Elyx

Belvedere Polish Rye Vodka

Boyd & Blair Potato Vodka

Death's Door Vodka

Grey Goose

Ketel One

Monopolowa

Reyka

Sobieski

St. George All Purpose Vodka

Stolichnaya

Tito's

Volstead

Wheatley

Wodka

Zodiac Potato Vodka

GIN

Aria Gin

Aviation Gin

Beefeater London Dry Gin

Bluecoat American Dry Gin

Bombay Sapphire

Boodles London Dry Gin

The Botanist Gin

Broker's Gin

Caorunn Scottish Gin

Citadelle Gin

Damrak Gin

Distillery No. 209 Gin

Finger Lakes Distilling Seneca Drums Gin

Fords Gin

Greenhook Ginsmiths

Hendrick's Gin

J. Rieger & Co. Midwestern Dry Gin

Junipero Gin

Martin Miller's Gin

Monkey 47

Old Raj

Plymouth Gin

Reisetbauer Blue Gin

Sipsmith London Dry Gin

St. Augustine New World Gin

St. George Terroir and Dry Rye Gins

Tanqueray and Tanqueray No. 10

Two James Old Cockney Gin

Ventura Spirits Wilder Gin

TEQUILA

Arette

Casa Dragones

Cazadores

Chamucos

Corralejo

Don Julio

El Charro

El Jimador

El Tesoro

Espolòn

Fortaleza

Fuenteseca

Gran Centenario

Herradura

Olmeca Altos

Partida

Pueblo Viejo

Siembra Azul/
Siembra Valles

Siete Leguas

Suerte

Tapatio

Tequila Ocho

MEZCAL

Alipus

Del Maguey

Derrumbes

Don Amado

El Jolgorio

El Pelotón de la Muerte

Fidencio

Ilegal

La Niña del Mezcal

Leyenda

Mayalen

Mezcal Vago

Mezcalero

Nuestra Soledad

Pierde Almas

RUM

7 Sirens

10 Cane

Angostura

Appleton Estate

Banks

Caña Brava

Diplomático

Don Q

El Dorado

Hamilton

Matusalem

Old Monk Pampero

Plantation

Privateer

Ron Zacapa

Santa Teresa

Scarlet Ibis

Smith & Cross

Wray & Nephew

PISCO

BarSol

Campo de Encanto

Capel

Control C

Huamaní

Macchu Pisco

Piscologia

Pisco Portón

COGNAC AND
OTHER BRANDY

Cardenal Mendoza

Frapin

Germain-Robin

Hine

Meukow Cognac

Park

Paul Beau

Pierre Ferrand

Rémy Martin

Continued >

RYE

Few

George Dickel

High West

James Oliver

Jim Beam Pre-Prohibition

Leopold Bros.

Michter's

Old Overholt

Pikesville Rye

Rittenhouse

Sazerac

WhistlePig

Wild Turkey 101

Willett

Workhorse Rye

BOURBON

Ancient Age

Booker's

Buffalo Trace

Eagle Rare

Elijah Craig

Evan Williams

Four Roses

Heaven Hill

Henry McKenna

Hirsch

Larceny

Maker's Mark

Medley Bros.

Michter's

Noah's MIll

Old Bardstown

Old Forester

Smooth Ambler

Widow Jane

W.L. Weller

SCOTCH

Aberlour

Auchentoshan

Balvenie

Bank Note

Campbeltown Loch

Compass Box Great King Street

Cutty Sark Prohibition

Dewar's

Famous Grouse and Black Grouse

Glenlivet

Highland Park

Isle of Skye

Lagavulin

Macallan

McClelland's

Oban

Pig's Nose

Springbank

Talisker

Teacher's

ACKNOWLEDGMENTS

There are few communities as generous as the bar community, and I owe thanks to hundreds of bartenders who have shared their insights and recipes with me over the years. I am so grateful to every bartender in this book: Kaitlyn Stewart, Sarah Rosner, Tommy Quimby, Bethany Kocak, Matthew McKinley Campbell, Arnaud Dissais, Julia Momose, Michael Neff, Shannon Tebay Sidle, Chris Morris, Kristina Magro, Tom Lindstedt, Brian Griffiths, Kate Bolton, Frank Cisneros, Collin Nicholas, Elsa Taylor, Christopher Longoria, Keli Rivers, Andrew Moore, Sother Teague, Karen Fu, Laura Newman, Ben Potts, Heather Sang, Benjamin Amberg, T. Cole Newton, Pilar Vree, Nicholas Bennett, Christopher Lowder, Kamil Foltan, Alan Ruesga-Pelayo, Ran Duan, Chelan Finney, Gabriella Mlynarczyk, Chad Hauge, Mindy Kucan, Justin Elliot, Adam James Sarkis, Jesse Carr, John McCarthy, Jeremy Simpson, Shaun Gordon, Shaun Traxler, Jason Saura, Liam Odien, A. Minetta Gould, Tiffany Hernandez, Nathan Shearer, Darwin Pornel, Nathaniel Smith, Nick Meyer, Matt Friedlander, Anna Moss, Alex Fletcher, Jesse Cyr, Laura Bellucci, Greg Innocent, Patrick Poelvoorde, David Perez, Caitlin Laman, Andrew M. Volk, Trevor Frye, Chris Amirault, Dee Ann Quinones, John Holzinger, Thomas Spaeth, Brandon Presbury, Benjamin Schiller, Zach Lynch, Lynnette Marrero, Jared Hirsch, Zac Overman, Jenna Jones, and Jordan Felix.

It was a dream to work with photographer extraordinaire Kelly Puleio and her entire team: producer Tamara Costa, stylist Maxwell Smith, bartenders Brian Barnett and Christina Cabrera, and assistants Nicola Parisi and Keri Mendonça.

I had no idea that this book would come to be when I sat down to share a massive cocktail in a pineapple with Emily Timberlake, but I'm so glad we ordered that piña colada. And thanks to the rest of the Ten Speed crew, including Ashley Lima, Hope Meng, David Hawk, and Jane Chinn. Thank you to my agent, Alison Fargis, for making it all happen, and fast.

Thanks to my parents and my in-laws for encouraging me to make the leap, and to Charlotte Towery, Bridget Veltri, and Eva Blehm, who tirelessly took Minna to visit the duck and the bunny while I tested recipes. Thanks to testers Emma Christensen, Mike Reis, Lauren Duffy Lastowka, Sasha Shusteff, Joe Ruvel, Kristen Sahler, and everyone else who gave these drinks a try.

My deepest gratitude to Ed Levine and the amazing folks of Serious Eats, past and present. I owe you an umbrella drink one of these days.

And to Matt, thank you for your humor, your patience, your enthusiasm, your calm presence, and your brilliant mind. In the end, it's not the drinks that make the cocktail hour great.

INDEX

Library of Congress Cataloging-in-Publication Data

Names: Hoffman, Maggie, author. | Puleio, Kelly, photographer.
Title: The one-bottle cocktail : more than 80 recipes with fresh ingredients
    and a single spirit / Maggie Hoffman ; photographs by Kelly Puleio.
Description: First edition. | New York : Ten Speed Press, [2017] | Includes
    bibliographical references and index.
Identifiers: LCCN 2017026604 (print) | LCCN 2017029753 (ebook)
Subjects: LCSH: Cocktails. | Alcoholic beverages. | LCGFT: Cookbooks.
Classification: LCC TX951 (ebook) | LCC TX951 .H62 2017 (print) | DDC
    641.87/4—dc23
LC record available at https://lccn.loc.gov/2017026604

Hardcover ISBN: 978-0-399-58004-8
eBook ISBN: 978-0-399-58005-5

Printed in China

Design by Hope Meng
Cover design by Ashley Lima
Styling by Maxwell Smith

10 9 8 7 6 5 4 3 2 1

First Edition